en français

Lɪɪ
Language Immersion Institute Series

en français
Rapid Success in French for Beginners

Marc Bendali and Marie-Paule Mahoney
Series Editor: Professor Henry Urbanski, Ph.D.
State University of New York at New Paltz

McGraw·Hill
New York   Chicago   San Francisco   Lisbon   London   Madrid   Mexico City
Milan   New Delhi   San Juan   Seoul   Singapore   Sydney   Toronto

Library of Congress Cataloging-in-Publication Data

Bendali, Marc.
    En français : rapid success in French for beginners / Marc Bendali and Marie-Paule Mahoney.
        p.   cm.
    English and French.
    ISBN 0-07-140649-2 (pbk.) 0-07-140648-4 (package)
    1. French language—Textbooks for foreign speakers—English.
 I. Mahoney, Marie-Paule. II. Title.

PC2129.E5E38 2003
448.2'421—dc21   2003042141

1 2 3 4 5 6 7 8 9 0 AGM/AGM 2 1 0 9 8 7 6 5 4 3

Package ISBN 0-07-140648-4
Book ISBN 0-07-140649-2

In the same series:
En español, Graciela España
In italiano, Sandra Immerso

Contents

À l'hôtel · *At the hotel* 80

Au Procope · *At the Procope* 99

La visite de Paris · *Touring Paris* 118

Randonnée à travers la France · *Roaming across France* 134

Provinces de France · *French provinces* 150

Introduction

Since 1981 the Language Immersion Institute, located at the State University of New York at New Paltz, has provided foreign language courses for more than 40,000 participants from all walks of life. The Institute's purpose has always been to proliferate foreign language study among adult learners through creative methods and programs that complement their busy work schedules and help them acquire proficiency in the shortest time possible.

The Immersion approach is predicated on the idea that intensive language study creates a highly effective and exciting learning environment that is congenial and non-threatening, and in which confidence in speaking ability is quickly attained. This is especially important in our rapidly shrinking world, where communication skills are vital. In the context of the global village we have become, the Language Immersion Institute offers innovative ways to study foreign languages, including English as a Second Language.

The mission of the Language Immersion Institute is threefold:

1. To make language study accessible and convenient to the adult learner through intensive courses that provide survival skills and practical conversational skills at all levels, thereby addressing the needs of persons beyond the secondary school level.

2. To dispel the misconception that language learning is a formidable task by dividing the learning process into small, progressive modules in which the learner discovers that acquiring language skills can be an achievable goal and an enjoyable endeavor.

3. To provide a real-life learning environment, in addition to the classroom, through overseas courses and other off-campus classes that stimulate the learner to use the language in a natural, non-academic setting.

This course series, including *En français*, is one way the Institute strives to bring foreign language study to the adult learner. Written by native speakers with many years of experience teaching at the Language Immersion Institute, the programs cover Elementary Levels I and II, the equivalent of six weekend courses or two semesters of study. As important as content, the programs also reflect the spirit of classes at the Language Immersion Institute. The audio recordings, a key component of the courses, were recorded in New Paltz by Institute teachers—not actors—to convey the infectious vitality that imbues the classes at the LII.

I hope you find studying French with this program a rewarding and inspiring experience.

Professor Henry Urbanski
Distinguished Service Professor of Russian,
Founder and Director of the Language Immersion Institute

How to use this course

This course is designed to help you master speaking French in real-life situations by learning vocabulary in context, basic grammar, and helpful cultural information.

The course is presented in nine chapters. Each chapter contains three dialogues, followed by a list of new vocabulary (**Petit lexique**) used in the dialogue and additional vocabulary (**Extension de vocabulaire**) related to the subject presented, but not used in the dialogue. Each dialogue introduces new expressions or structures, as well as new vocabulary used in context. To help you understand these new expressions, explanations of their use (**Compréhension et expressions**) and associated grammar (**Structure grammaticale**) are provided. Written exercises in this book and audio exercises on the CD offer ample opportunity to practice the material. As an optional aid, the text of the audio practices and the audio exercise questions is included in the book. This way you will hear, repeat, and write the new structures until you master them.

Most chapters contain a section called **Common pitfalls**, where you will hear a student and teacher interact on the recording. This section is intended to help you review the new material and to show you some typical mistakes to avoid. Also on the recording, the section called **Let's take a plunge!** poses questions to be answered as in a spontaneous conversation. Returning to this book, **Vive la différence!** provides cultural information that will help you understand the language from a personal perspective. Finally, at the end of each chapter, **How to make it sound French** will help you master pronunciation.

At the back of the book is the Answer key, where you will find the solution for each written exercise (answers to audio exercises are on the recording), so you can be sure at all times that you know the right answer. **Grammar summary** is a synopsis of selected grammatical aspects covered in the program for quick reference. And the French-English glossary and English-French glossary allow you to find the French or English equivalents of all the vocabulary presented.

In order to understand and retain the material, the following approach is suggested.

1. Open your book to the beginning of the chapter you are about to study. Read the chapter's objective and insert the CD.
2. Listen to the first dialogue, then stop the recording.
3. Read the dialogue in the book, looking up the words you don't know in the **Petit lexique** section. Study the new vocabulary before you proceed.
4. Replay the dialogue, pausing the CD to allow you to repeat each segment. Repeat this as many times as necessary to both recognize the vocabulary and pronounce the words clearly and with ease.
5. Following the instructions on the CD or in the book, progress through the grammatical explanations and the exercises in the book and on the CD until you come to the next dialogue.

    It is important to work at your own pace and take all the time you need to practice. Do not proceed to the next exercise until you feel you have mastered the one you just completed. Going over an audio exercise as many times as necessary is the key to progress. Also, try to imitate the speakers' intonation and pronunciation as closely as possible.
6. Once you have mastered the vocabulary and the exercises, move on to the next dialogue and repeat steps one to five.

After you have completed the course, insert the third CD. This CD covers all elements that you have studied; you may use it to review, strengthen, and assess your knowledge of French. It may also be used independently, to help you brush up on your French before a trip to France or a Francophone region, or before a business meeting or a social or cultural event.

Cognates

What are "cognates"? Notice that the word shares the same stem or root as "recognize." Indeed, there are plenty of words that are recognizable in French because they share the same root or stem as their English equivalents. A letter or two may differ between the two languages, but the meaning is basically the same. These words are called "cognates." There are exceptions, of course, for French would not be French without exceptions!

Let's look at some cognates.

commander	*to command, to order*
pratiquer	*to practice*
choisir	*to choose*
établir	*to establish*
presser	*to press*

There is a group of cognates that are virtually identical in both languages; it is the group of "-tion" nouns. Words ending in "-tion" will be spelled the same, or nearly the same, in French and English. Except for a few words called **faux amis** ("false friends"), these cognates have identical meanings. The only difference is the pronunciation, in particular the suffix "-tion," which is pronounced /shun/ in English and /see-on/ in French.

information	*information*
éducation	*education*
nation	*nation*
animation	*animation*

Practice

The following activity is not a test but a practical exercise to help you become more familiar with word recognition and to build self-confidence. You can repeat this exercise on a regular basis, even once a week. Select a French text from your textbook, a book or magazine, or the Internet; look for words you think you recognize because they are similar to words you know in English. Underline at least ten words, and try to guess their meaning. Then check your accuracy with a bilingual dictionary. You will quickly discover that you know more French vocabulary than you thought you did.

As an example, look at the following paragraph and underline the words whose meaning you can guess because they look like English words. Don't attempt to understand the meaning of the text, and don't use a dictionary or reference book.

> Pierre entre dans un restaurant et décide de s'installer à une table près de la fenêtre. Le garçon arrive et lui demande s'il désire voir le menu. Pierre répond que ce n'est pas nécessaire parce qu'il sait ce qu'il veut commander.

Once you have underlined the words you recognize, list them below and write what you believe to be their English equivalents. There are twelve cognates.

FRENCH	ENGLISH
1. entre	enter
2. restaurant	restaurant
3. décide	decide
4. table	table
5. arrive	arrive
6. demande	demand
7. desire	wish
8. menu	menu
9. respond	respond
10. command	order
11.	
12.	

Now, try to make sense of the paragraph.

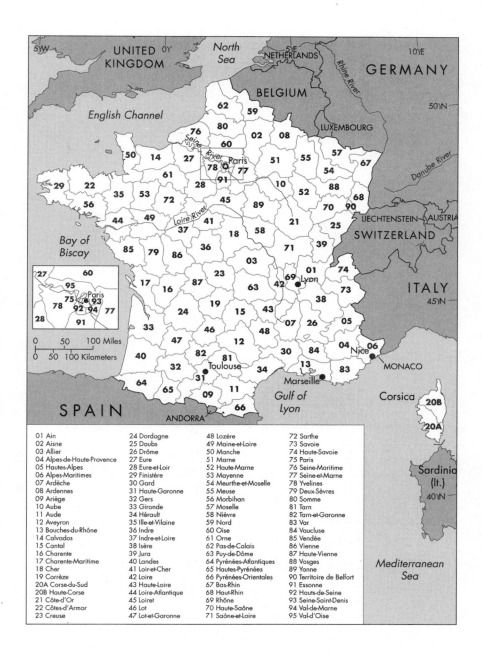

01 Ain	24 Dordogne	48 Lozère	72 Sarthe
02 Aisne	25 Doubs	49 Maine-et-Loire	73 Savoie
03 Allier	26 Drôme	50 Manche	74 Haute-Savoie
04 Alpes-de-Haute-Provence	27 Eure	51 Marne	75 Paris
05 Hautes-Alpes	28 Eure-et-Loir	52 Haute-Marne	76 Seine-Maritime
06 Alpes-Maritimes	29 Finistère	53 Mayenne	77 Seine-et-Marne
07 Ardèche	30 Gard	54 Meurthe-et-Moselle	78 Yvelines
08 Ardennes	31 Haute-Garonne	55 Meuse	79 Deux-Sèvres
09 Ariège	32 Gers	56 Morbihan	80 Somme
10 Aube	33 Gironde	57 Moselle	81 Tarn
11 Aude	34 Hérault	58 Nièvre	82 Tarn-et-Garonne
12 Aveyron	35 Ille-et-Vilaine	59 Nord	83 Var
13 Bouches-du-Rhône	36 Indre	60 Oise	84 Vaucluse
14 Calvados	37 Indre-et-Loire	61 Orne	85 Vendée
15 Cantal	38 Isère	62 Pas-de-Calais	86 Vienne
16 Charente	39 Jura	63 Puy-de-Dôme	87 Haute-Vienne
17 Charente-Maritime	40 Landes	64 Pyrénées-Atlantiques	88 Vosges
18 Cher	41 Loir-et-Cher	65 Hautes-Pyrénées	89 Yonne
19 Corrèze	42 Loire	66 Pyrénées-Orientales	90 Territoire de Belfort
20A Corse-du-Sud	43 Haute-Loire	67 Bas-Rhin	91 Essonne
20B Haute-Corse	44 Loire-Atlantique	68 Haut-Rhin	92 Hauts-de-Seine
21 Côte-d'Or	45 Loiret	69 Rhône	93 Seine-Saint-Denis
22 Côtes-d'Armor	46 Lot	70 Haute-Saône	94 Val-de-Marne
23 Creuse	47 Lot-et-Garonne	71 Saône-et-Loire	95 Val-d'Oise

◄ 1 ►

Bonjour
Hello

OBJECTIVE

In this chapter, you will greet French native speakers and introduce yourself. You will express who you are, where you are, and where you come from. You will get to know some of the rules of *savoir faire* and also start to learn the names of professions and nationalities.

DIALOGUE 1
À New Paltz · *In New Paltz*

Let us meet our three American friends from New York, the three
"J"s: Mr. Jones, Jeremy, and Jennifer. Mr. Jones is a doctor, Jeremy
a basketball player, and Jennifer a journalist. Their dream is to
learn French and visit France. Let's join them on their adventure,
first to learn French at the Immersion Institute in New Paltz.

*Faisons connaissance avec nos trois amis américains de New York:
M. Jones, Jennifer et Jeremy. M. Jones est médecin, Jeremy est joueur
de basket et Jennifer est journaliste. Les trois «J» sont à l'Institut
d'Immersion de New Paltz pour apprendre le français.*

M. JONES	Bonjour les amis, comment allez-vous?
JEREMY	Ça va, et vous, monsieur Jones?
M. JONES	Bien merci, et vous Jennifer?
JENNIFER	Pas mal. Jeremy, ça va?
JEREMY	Comme ci comme ça. Excusez-moi, je suis pressé.
M. JONES ET JENNIFER	Au revoir, à tout à l'heure.

Petit lexique

à tout à l'heure	*see you later*
l'ami (*m.*)	*friend*
les amis (*m.pl.*)	*friends*
au revoir	*good-bye*
bien	*well*
bonjour	*hello; good morning; good afternoon*
bonsoir	*hello; good evening; good-bye*
ça va? (*familiar*)	*how are you?*
comme ci comme ça	*so-so*
Comment allez-vous? (*formal*)	*How are you?*
et	*and*
excusez-moi	*excuse me; sorry*
je suis pressé(e)	*I am in a hurry*
merci	*thank you*

Madame (Mesdames)	*Mrs.; madam; lady (ladies)*
Mademoiselle	*miss; lady*
Mesdemoiselles	*misses; ladies*
Monsieur	*Mr.; sir*
Messieurs	*sirs; gentlemen*
pas mal	*not bad*
vous	*you*

◄ 1.3 ►
Compréhension et expressions

Greetings

Bonjour · *Hello, Good morning, Good afternoon*

In France, ways of greeting depend on the time of day. For most parts of the day you will say **Bonjour!**

| bonjour | *hello; good morning; good afternoon* |

When talking to someone you do not know very well, add a title of respect at the end of your greeting.

Monsieur	*for a man*
Madame	*for an older or married woman*
Mademoiselle	*for a young, unmarried woman or girl*

Bonsoir · *Hello, Good evening*

Toward the end of the day, you will say **Bonsoir!**

| bonsoir | *hello; good evening; good-bye (at night)* |

Messieurs-dames · *Ladies and gentlemen*

If you are talking to more than one person, **Monsieur** becomes **Messieurs**, **Madame** becomes **Mesdames**, and **Mademoiselle** becomes **Mesdemoiselles**. For a mixed group (men and women), just use **Messieurs-dames**.

Bonjour Messieurs.	*Hello, gentlemen.*
Bonsoir Mesdames.	*Hello, ladies.*
Bonjour Mesdemoiselles.	*Hello, ladies.*
Bonsoir Messieurs-dames.	*Hello, ladies and gentlemen.*

Salut · *Hi*

Salut is the informal way used to greet friends at any time (whether meeting or leaving).

Salut Paul! Ça va? (*very informal*)	*Hi, Paul! How are things?*

Your response to this question may vary. Notice that the use of the first two words **je vais** (formal) and **ça va** (informal) is optional.

(Je vais/Ça va) très bien merci.	*(I am/Things are) very well, thank you.*
(Je vais/Ça va) bien merci.	*(I am/Things are) well, thank you.*
(Je vais/Ça va) pas mal.	*(I am/Things are) not bad.*
Pas très bien.	*Not too well.*
Comme ci comme ça.	*So-so.*
Mal.	*Badly, terribly.*
Très mal.	*Very badly.*

Your response will be followed by an inquiry about the other person's health using **et vous?** ("and you?", formal) or **et toi?** ("and you?", informal).

Farewells

Bonne nuit · *Good night*

We have already learned how to say **Bonsoir** and **Salut** when departing. At night we say **Bonne nuit** when departing or going to bed.

Bonne nuit papa.	*Good night, daddy.*
Bonne nuit maman.	*Good night, mom.*

However, the most common farewell in French is **au revoir**.

Au revoir Madame Ricard.	*Good-bye, Mrs. Ricard.*
Au revoir Mesdemoiselles.	*Good-bye, misses (young ladies).*

Adieu · *Good-bye*

Adieu is commonly used in Switzerland and Canada to say "good-bye." However, in France **adieu** is normally used when parting for a long time or forever.

    Adieu Julien.   *Good-bye, Julien.*

In Canada, **bonjour** can also be used when leaving.

Other common expressions are used to specify when you will see the people again.

    À tout à l'heure.   *See you later.*
    À demain.   *See you tomorrow.*
    À bientôt.   *See you soon.*

 ◄ **1.4** ►

Audio practice

Listen to the recording for practice in listening to and repeating greetings.

 ◄ **1.5** ►

Audio exercise

Listen to the recording to practice greeting people according to the time of the day using **Bonjour** or **Bonsoir** and stating **Mademoiselle, Madame, Monsieur**, or the plural form if there is more than one: **Mesdemoiselles, Mesdames, Messieurs**. You will use **Messieurs-dames** for a group of women and men. Then, repeat the correct response after the speaker.

EXAMPLE

PROMPT   It is 7 A.M. and you meet Madame Rocher.
RESPONSE   Bonjour Madame.

◄ 1.6 ►
Audio exercise

On the recording, greet the different people in the illustrations below according to the time of day.

EXAMPLE

RESPONSE   Bonsoir Monsieur.

1.

2.

3.

4.

5.

6.

◄ 1.7 ►
DIALOGUE 2
Présentations · *Introductions*

The following conversation between M. Pierre Durand and Mme Jacqueline Berger will help you introduce yourself when you meet people for the first time. The question asks "What is your name?" **Comment vous appelez-vous?** (literally, "What do you call yourself?") and you reply **Je m'appelle** _____ and give your name. Introductions are generally followed by saying **Enchanté(e)**, meaning "delighted."

PIERRE	Bonjour Madame, je m'appelle Pierre Durand. Et vous, comment vous appelez-vous?
JACQUELINE	Je m'appelle Jacqueline Berger. Enchantée, Monsieur.
PIERRE	Enchanté, Madame.
JACQUELINE	Vous êtes d'où, Monsieur?
PIERRE	Je suis de Nice. Et vous, Madame?
JACQUELINE	Moi, je suis de Bordeaux.

Vous êtes d'où? and **D'où êtes-vous?** both mean "Where do you come from?"

◄ 1.8 ►
Petit lexique

à	*at; in; to*
Comment vous appelez-vous?	*What is your name?*
de	*from; of*
enchanté(e)	*delighted*
être	*to be*
je m'appelle _____	*my name is _____*
moi	*me, I*
la présentation	*introduction*
où	*where*
Vous êtes d'où?	*Where do you come from?*

◄ 1.9 ►
Compréhension et expressions

Salutations et savoir faire · *Greetings and protocol*

The French tend to be very formal when they meet people for the first time. When introducing two different people, they will say, for example:

Permettez-moi de vous présenter Madame Villard.	*Allow me to introduce to you Mrs. Villard.*

or, in a less formal way,

Je vous présente Mme Villard.

When introduced to another person, you say:

Je suis enchanté(e). *I'm pleased to meet you., Delighted.*

or simply

Enchanté(e)!

To express gratitude and thanks, you say the following.

Merci. OR Merci beaucoup. *Thank you. OR Thank you very much.*

The reply to **Merci** is **De rien** (literally, "for nothing"), or in other words, "you're welcome."

Pardon · *Excuse me, Sorry*

When someone holds the door open to let you pass through, you thank the person by saying **pardon** as you pass through the door.

Vous êtes d'où? · *Where are you from? (You are from where?)*

To express where you are from or where you come from, you put **de** or **d'** (when it precedes a vowel or a silent **h**) before the name of the town.

Je suis de New York. *I am from New York.*

Il est d'où? *Where is he from?*
Il est de Boston. *He is from Boston.*

Elle est d'où? *Where is she from?*
Elle est de Londres. *She is from London.*

  ◄ **1.10** ►
Audio exercise

Imagine you are on a plane, and you introduce yourself to the person sitting next to you. You are the person depicted in each picture below. Listen to the recording. You will be asked your name and where you are from, then answer the questions.

EXAMPLE

Pierre Durand (Bordeaux)

PROMPT   Comment vous appelez-vous?
RESPONSE   Je m'appelle Pierre Durand.
PROMPT   Vous êtes d'où?
RESPONSE   Je suis de Bordeaux.

1. Jacqueline Berger
   (Lille)

2. Peter Carson
   (Montréal)

3. Arnaud Gérard
   (Lausanne)

4. Christian Dupuis
   (Strasbourg)

5. Caroline Vilbois
   (Nantes)

6. André Latour
   (Alger)

 ◄ **1.11** ►
Exercise

Listen to the recording, where you will be asked to name the person in each picture (see above) and to state where he or she comes from.

EXAMPLE

RESPONSE   Elle s'appelle Jacqueline Berger. Elle est de Lille.

◄ **1.12** ►

Structure grammaticale

être · *to be*

When we say **Jeremy est joueur de basket**, we are expressing a state of being, the same as when we say **M. Jones, Jennifer et Jeremy sont américains**, we are expressing that they are American. We see that the verb expressing this state is **est** or **sont**, two forms of the verb **être** ("to be"). Let's look at all the forms.

je suis	Je **suis** français.	*I am French.*
tu es	Tu **es** américaine.	*You are American.*
il est	Il **est** docteur.	*He is a doctor.*
elle est	Elle **est** journaliste.	*She is a journalist.*
nous sommes	Nous **sommes** étudiants.	*We are students.*
vous êtes	Vous **êtes** fatigué(s).	*You are tired.*
ils sont	Ils **sont** européens.	*They are European.*
elles sont	Elles **sont** africaines.	*They are African.*

To give the name of a profession, you add the name of the profession directly after the form of the verb **être** ("to be") without including the indefinite article **un** or **une** ("a").

John **est** étudiant.	*John is a student.*
Il **est** étudiant.	*He is a student.*
Jennifer **est** journaliste.	*Jennifer is a journalist.*
Elle **est** journaliste.	*She is a journalist.*

To give the name of a nationality, you add the name of the nationality directly after the form of the verb **être** ("to be").

M. Jones, Jennifer et Jeremy sont américains.	*Mr. Jones, Jennifer, and Jeremy are American.*
Ils sont américains.	*They are American.*
Jennifer et Marie sont américaines.	*Jennifer and Marie are American.*
Elles sont américaines.	*They are American.*

Subject pronouns

When one talks to or about people, subject pronouns are used to replace their names. Subject pronouns are either singular, when they replace one person, or plural, when they replace more than one. Some subject pronouns also reflect gender: masculine (*m.*) and feminine (*f.*).

Here are the principal subject pronouns.

SINGULAR		PLURAL	
je	*I*	nous	*we*
tu/vous	*you*	vous	*you*
il (*m.*)	*he/it*	ils (*m.*)	*they*
elle (*f.*)	*she/it*	elles (*f.*)	*they*

NOTE: **Tu** is the "you" form of the personal pronoun in French when you are addressing a person informally.

Vous is the "you" form when you are addressing someone formally or when you are addressing more than one person at a time.

 ◀ **1.13** ▶
Audio practice

Être is a basic verb. Listen to the recording and repeat, but this time say which town different people are in, simply by putting **à** before the name of the town.

1. Je suis à Paris.   *I am in Paris.*
2. Nous sommes à Ivry.   *We are in Ivry.*
3. Tu es à Dijon.   *You are in Dijon.*
4. Vous êtes à Chinon.   *You are in Chinon.*
5. Il est à Calais.   *He is in Calais.*
6. Ils sont à Roubaix.   *They are in Roubaix.*
7. Elle est à Alençon.   *She is in Alençon.*
8. Ils sont à Besançon.   *They are in Besançon.*

◀ **1.14** ▶
Exercise

Complete the following sentences with the appropriate pronoun.

EXAMPLE   __Je__ suis américain.

1. _____ est étudiant.
2. _____ sommes américains.
3. _____ sont à la terrasse des Deux Magots à Paris.
4. _____ suis professeur de français.

5. _____ êtes en Italie.

6. _____ es fatigué.

7. _____ sont américaines.

8. _____ es intelligent.

9. _____ est intelligente.

◄ 1.15 ►
Exercise

Complete the following sentences, using the appropriate form of the verb **être**.

EXAMPLE   Vous _êtes_ à Dijon.

1. Jennifer _____ journaliste.

2. Jeremy et John _____ américains.

3. Je _____ à la terrasse de Rockefeller Center.

4. Tu _____ au musée du Louvre.

5. Marie-Paule et Marc _____ à la terrasse du Fouquet's.

6. Nous _____ étudiants de français.

7. Vous _____ au jardin du Luxembourg.

8. Il _____ étudiant en médecine.

9. Mathilde _____ réceptionniste.

10. Elle _____ en vacances en Normandie.

◄ 1.16 ►
DIALOGUE 3
Adieu! · *Good-bye!*

Adieu is commonly used in Switzerland to say "good-bye." However, in France, **adieu** is used when we leave somebody for a long time or forever.

Our friend Jeremy and his French girlfriend, Marie-France, were passionately in love. Sadly, Marie-France has decided to break off the relationship.

Notre ami Jeremy et sa petite amie française Marie-France s'aimaient passionnément. Malheureusement Marie-France a décidé de rompre.

JEREMY	À tout à l'heure, Marie-France.
MARIE-FRANCE	Non, Jeremy.
JEREMY	Marie-France, mon amour, à demain.
MARIE-FRANCE	Non, Jeremy.
JEREMY	Marie-France, ma chérie, ne me quitte pas. À bientôt!
MARIE-FRANCE	Non, Jeremy. Adieu! Adieu! Adieu!

◄ **1.17** ►
Petit lexique

adieu	*good-bye, farewell*
l'amour (*m.*)	*love*
chéri/chérie	*darling*
mon/ma	*my*
ne me quitte pas	*don't leave me*
non	*no*

◄ **1.18** ►
Exercise

Many names of professions are similar in French and in English; they are cognates. See if you can identify the following ones. Write the equivalent word in English.

1. plombier _____
2. dentiste _____
3. réceptionniste _____
4. électricien _____
5. mécanicien _____
6. technicien _____
7. vétérinaire _____
8. secrétaire _____
9. docteur _____
10. professeur _____

◄ 1.19 ►
Common pitfalls

Listen on the recording to a class conversation between a student and the teacher. The student misunderstands the false cognate **merci**, which means "thank you," not "mercy."

◄ 1.20 ►
Let's take a plunge!

Using what you have learned in this chapter, take the part of one of the speakers in a spontaneous conversation. You'll be asked to say hello, how you're feeling, what your name is, what your nationality is, what your job is, where you're from, and—finally—good-bye.

◄ 1.21 ►
Vive la différence!

Greetings

In France, you shake hands not just when you are being introduced to people for the first time, but every time you meet or say good-bye to them. Family members and close friends kiss each other on both cheeks, sometimes three or four times!

Unless you are very familiar with a person, you will always address him/her as **Monsieur**, **Madame**, or **Mademoiselle**.

What makes the French *French*

This question can never be answered adequately. The French have the reputation of being difficult to get to know. They have an eternal love for the "Made in France" label, from baguettes to "real" champagne, French cinema, and, above all, their language. They can be so extremely polite and formal in many ways, while appearing to be abrupt in others. On entering a French shop, one greets other shoppers, who may be total strangers, with **Bonjour, Madame** or **Bonjour, Monsieur**.

Le Coq

The rooster has been the national emblem of France for over two thousand years, ever since the country was known as Gaul. The Romans who invaded and colonized Gaul called its people the "Galli," plural for "Gallus," the Latin word for "rooster."

◄ **1.22** ►
How to make it sound French

The French tend to stress the last syllable of a word.

bon<u>jour</u>	bon<u>soir</u>	Mon<u>sieur</u>	Ma<u>dame</u>
Pa<u>ris</u>	mer<u>ci</u>	au re<u>voir</u>	à bien<u>tôt</u>

Plans de voyage
Travel plans

OBJECTIVE

In this chapter, you are planning to go to France, since your French studies are going so well! You want to find out about **les grands plaisirs**! Don't be shy in asking questions. If everything else fails, you can always talk about the weather. . . .

◄ 2.1 ►
DIALOGUE 1
Une idée · *An idea*

A little later that day, our three friends get toge
their French class.

Un peu plus tard, nos trois amis sont de nouveau en: .... *la*
classe de français.

JENNIFER   Et le français, les amis, ça marche?

JEREMY   Oui, ça marche bien! J'aime la classe de français. Regarde,
           voici le livre de français avec la cassette et le CD.

M. JONES   J'adore le français et je vais bientôt en France.

JENNIFER   En France! J'aime la France, j'adore Paris et les monuments
           historiques.

JEREMY   Paris? Moi aussi.

M. JONES   Alors on va ensemble!

JEREMY   Pourquoi pas? C'est une idée.

JENNIFER   L'idée est bonne!

◄ 2.2 ►
Petit lexique

adorer	*to love*
aimer	*to like; to love*
aller	*to go*
alors	*then*
avec	*with*
bientôt	*soon*
bon/bonne	*good*
la cassette	*cassette*
la classe	*class*
en	*in; to*
ensemble	*together*
le français	*French (language)*
la France	*France*
historique	*historic*
l'idée (*f.*)	*idea*
marcher	*to work; to function*
moi aussi	*so do I (literally, me too)*
le monument	*monument*
oui	*yes*

Pourquoi pas?	Why not?
regarder	to look at
voici	here is

Extension de vocabulaire

le bureau	desk
le cahier	notebook
la calculatrice	calculator
la cartouche	cartridge
le classeur	binder
le crayon	pencil
la feuille	sheet (of paper)
le livre	book
l'ordinateur (m.)	computer
le sac, le cartable	schoolbag
le stylo	ink (ballpoint) pen

◄ 2.3 ►
Compréhension et expressions

Ça marche · *It's going well*

The expression **ça marche** is a colloquial way to say that things are going well, or that everything is going the way you want it to.

Ça marche le français?	*How is your French going?*
Ça marche?, Ça va?	*How are you doing?*
La télévision marche bien.	*The TV is functioning/working well.*
Le CD marche bien.	*The CD works well.*
La Renault marche bien.	*The Renault runs well.*

NOTE: As you can see, **ça marche** can be substituted for **ça va**.

on · *one*

The pronoun **on** is the impersonal form equivalent to "one," "we," or "they" in English. It takes the third-person singular form of the verb.

On parle français.	*One speaks/We speak/They speak French.*
On va à Paris.	*We go to Paris.*
On adore les monuments historiques.	*We love historic monuments.*

◄ **2.4** ►

Structure grammaticale

Regular verbs

In English, the infinitive of verbs begins with "to," as in "to work" and "to speak." In French, the infinitive is expressed by the ending of the verb. There are three groups of regular verbs; their infinitives end in **-er**, **-ir**, and **-re**.

adorer	*to love, to like strongly*
choisir	*to choose*
vendre	*to sell*

You will notice that **adorer** ends in **-er**, **choisir** in **-ir**, and **vendre** in **-re**. The ending of the infinitive determines the conjugation of each of these verbs and all other verbs with the same endings.

Present tense of regular -*er* verbs

The largest group of regular verbs ends in **-er**. To conjugate these verbs, take the infinitive form of the verb, drop the **-er**, and add the endings according to the subject.

TRAVAILLER ("to work")

je travaille	*I work; I'm working*
tu travailles	*you work; you're working*
il/elle/on travaille	*he/she/it/one works;*
	he/she/it/one is working
nous travaill**ons**	*we work; we're working*
vous travaill**ez**	*you work; you're working*
ils/elles travaill**ent**	*they work; they're working*

NOTE: **Je travaille** and the other forms correspond to two expressions of the present tense in English: "I work" and "I am working."

All the other regular **-er** verbs follow the same pattern.

Here are some common **-er** verbs.

acheter	*to buy*
adorer	*to like a lot; to idolize*
aimer	*to like; to love*
commander	*to order*

commencer*	*to start*
détester	*to dislike; to detest*
écouter	*to listen*
étudier	*to study*
habiter	*to live*
jouer	*to play*
manger*	*to eat*
parler	*to speak*
regarder	*to look at, to watch*
réserver	*to reserve*
rêver	*to dream*
travailler	*to work*
visiter	*to visit (a place)*
voyager*	*to travel*

The verbs marked with an asterisk have a spelling change in the stem in the **nous** form of the present tense. A cedilla is added under the **c** at the end of the stem of **commencer: nous commençons**. An **e** is added after the **g** at the end of the stem in **manger** and **voyager: nous mangeons, nous voyageons**.

Forming a question

In spoken French, just as in English, a simple way to ask a question is to make a statement with a rising intonation.

Vous parlez français.	*You speak French.*
Vous parlez français?	*Do you speak French?*

◄ 2.5 ►
Audio practice

Note that the pronunciation for the endings of regular -er verbs is identical for **je, tu, il, elle, on, ils,** and **elles**. Listen to the recording and repeat.

Je regarde la télé.	*I am watching TV.*
Tu écoutes la musique.	*You are listening to music.*
Elle achète une bouteille de coca-cola.	*She is buying a bottle of Coca-Cola.*
Jeremy joue au basket.	*Jeremy is playing basketball.*
Nous travaillons à Paris.	*We work in Paris.*

Vous aimez les films d'action.	*You like action movies.*
Elles adorent le cinéma.	*They love the movies.*
On parle français à Montréal.	*French is spoken in Montreal.*

◄ 2.6 ►
Audio exercise

You will hear the infinitive form of the verb and the subject. Respond with the correct form of the verb, and repeat the correct response after the speaker.

EXAMPLE

PROMPT   parler (nous)

RESPONSE   Nous parlons.

◄ 2.7 ►
Audio exercise

Answer the questions on the recording in the affirmative, starting your answer with **Oui**.

EXAMPLE

PROMPT   Vous parlez français?

RESPONSE   Oui, je parle français.

◄ 2.8 ►
Exercise

Select the correct form of the verb, and complete the sentence.

EXAMPLE   Parle/parlons/parlez français.

Je _parle_ français.

1. Travaillez/travaille/travaillons au musée du Louvre

   Nous _____ au musée du Louvre.

2. Habitez/habitons/habitent à Dijon

   Paul et Valérie _____ à Dijon.

3. Joue/jouons/jouez de la guitare

   Vous _____ de la guitare.

4. Aimons/aimes/aimez la France

   Tu _____ la France.

5. Regardent/regardons/regardez la tour Eiffel

   Nous _____ la tour Eiffel.

6. Parle/parlons/parlez français

   On _____ français.

◀ 2.9 ▶
Exercise

Complete the following sentences with the correct form of the verb in parentheses.

1. Nous __*parlons*__ français avec le professeur dans la classe. (parler)

2. Je __*travaille*__ à Montréal. (travailler)

3. On __*aime*__ les films d'action. (aimer)

4. Vous __*adorez*__ la mousse au chocolat. (adorer)

5. Vous __*jouez*__ au tennis? (jouer)

6. Elle __*reservent*__ un billet pour le concert. (réserver) (billet, *ticket*)

7. On __*regarde*__ la télévision. (regarder)

8. Ils __*habitent*__ à Alger. (habiter)

9. Elles __*écoutent*__ le discours du président. (écouter) (discours, *speech*)

10. Tu __*commences*__ à parler français. (commencer)

◀ 2.10 ▶
DIALOGUE 2
Les grands plaisirs · *The pleasures of life*

While the verb "to adore" means "to love strongly" in English, in French **adorer** means "to like a lot" or "to idolize." In this conversation, Paule, Isabelle, and Michel express what they like and love.

Paule, Isabelle et Michel parlent de ce qu'ils aiment et de ce qu'ils adorent.

PAULE	J'aime beaucoup les éclairs, qu'est-ce que tu aimes?
ISABELLE	J'adore la mousse au chocolat, et toi Michel?
MICHEL	J'adore les films d'action et le jazz.
PAULE	Moi, j'adore le rap.

◄ 2.11 ►
Petit lexique

beaucoup	*a lot, very much*
grand	*big; tall; great*
moi	*I, myself, for my part*
▶ le plaisir	*pleasure*
◆ qu'est-ce que/qu'?	*what?*
◆ toi	*you, yourself (familiar), for your part*

In the dialogue, you probably recognized the word **éclair**, which is a French pastry. Here are other pastries and desserts with which you are probably familiar.

le café	*coffee*
le cappuccino	*cappuccino*
la crème	*cream*
la crème brûlée	*crème brûlée (a custard topped with caramelized sugar)*
la crêpe	*crêpe; pancake*
l'éclair (*m.*)	*éclair*
• le gâteau	*cake*
la mousse au chocolat	*chocolate mousse*
' la pâtisserie	*pastry*
• la pêche Melba	*peach Melba*
◆ le sorbet	*sherbet*
◆ la tarte aux fruits	*fruit pie*

◄ 2.12 ►
Structure grammaticale

Les articles définis · *Definite articles*

All French nouns (for both people and objects) are either masculine or feminine. The gender of a noun is indicated by an article.

le garçon	*the boy*	les garçons	*the boys*
la fille	*the girl*	les filles	*the girls*
le livre	*the book*	les livres	*the books*
la classe	*the class*	les classes	*the classes*
l'orange (*f.*)	*the orange*	les oranges	*the oranges*

The word for "the" has four different forms in French: **le**, **la**, **l'**, and **les**.

Before a singular noun

MASCULINE	le	*the*
FEMININE	la	*the*
MASCULINE/FEMININE	l'	*the* (when the noun starts with a vowel or silent **h**)

Before a plural noun

MASCULINE/FEMININE	les	*the*

In the dialogue, Jeremy says:

Voici le livre de français avec la cassette.	*Here is the French book with the cassette.*

Le livre is masculine and **la cassette** is feminine.

How to tell whether a noun is masculine or feminine

With some nouns it is obvious: **le garçon** ("the boy") is masculine and **la fille** ("the girl") is feminine. However, with **le livre** and **la cassette**, there is no logical reason. Therefore, when learning French nouns, you must memorize them with the definite article **le** or **la**.

Note that when you want to use a pronoun for a thing or an object, you will use **il** ("it") to replace a masculine singular noun and **elle** ("it") for a feminine singular noun. In the same way, **ils** ("they") is used to replace masculine plural nouns and **elles** ("they") feminine plural nouns.

Le café est chaud?	*The coffee is hot?*
Oui, il est très chaud.	*Yes, it is very hot.*
La classe de français est bonne?	*The French class is good?*
Oui, elle est excellente.	*Yes, it is excellent.*

Les éclairs sont au chocolat ou à la vanille?	*Are the éclairs chocolate or vanilla?*
Ils sont au chocolat.	*They are chocolate.*
Les crêpes sont à l'abricot?	*Are they apricot crêpes?*
Oui, elles sont à l'abricot.	*Yes, they are made with apricots.*

It is important to remember that the masculine always supersedes the feminine in French. Therefore, even if you have several feminine persons or objects and only one masculine person or object, the pronoun will be masculine plural.

◄ 2.13 ►
Audio exercise

On the recording, you will be prompted to answer the following questions in the affirmative.

EXAMPLE

PROMPT   Tu aimes les éclairs? (Yes, I love éclairs.)

RESPONSE   Oui, j'adore les éclairs.

◄ 2.14 ►
Exercise

Complete the following sentences with the appropriate article: **le, la, l',** or **les.**

1. _les_ crayons sont sur _la_ table.

2. Je regarde _la_ cassette vidéo en français.

3. _les_ amis visitent _les_ monuments historiques.

4. _l'_ idée est bonne.

5. _Les_ éclairs sont délicieux.

6. _le_ livre, _le_ stylo et _les_ feuilles sont dans _le_ cartable.

7. En France, on termine _le_ repas avec _la_ salade. (terminer, *to end*; repas, *meal*)

8. _la_ télévision marche bien.

◄ **2.15** ►
Exercice

Complete the following sentences with the correct form of the verb and the appropriate definite article.

1. Elle _aime_ _la_ mousse au chocolat?
(aimer)

2. _Les_ étudiants _utilisent_ _les_ calculatrices.
(utiliser)

3. _Le_ professeur et _les_ étudiants _parlent_ français. (parler)

4. Jeremy et Jennifer _adorent_ _la_ France. (adorer)

5. _La_ crème brûlée et _le_ cappuccino _sont_ _les_ desserts préférés de Jeremy. (être)

◄ **2.16** ►
DIALOGUE 3
Quel temps fait-il? • *What's the weather like?*

The three "J"s are seriously considering going to France together. It is now springtime and they are discussing what the weather is like there.

Les trois amis pensent sérieusement à aller en France ensemble. C'est le printemps et ils parlent du temps qu'il fait là-bas.

M. JONES   Nous sommes au printemps. Il fait froid à Paris?

JENNIFER   Non, mais il pleut souvent. Le matin et le soir il fait un peu frais.

JEREMY   Il neige?

JENNIFER   Jamais. Les hirondelles chantent et les marronniers sont en fleurs. Paris est magnifique!

JEREMY   J'aime le printemps mais j'adore l'été. J'aime nager et marcher sur la plage...

JENNIFER   ... et jouer au basket.

JEREMY   Oui... et j'adore le ski en hiver et la bicyclette en automne.

M. JONES   Eh! les amis, c'est oui ou non pour le voyage en France?

◄ 2.17 ►
Petit lexique

l'automne (*m.*)	*autumn, fall*
la bicyclette	*bicycle*
eh	*hey*
eh bien	*well*
l'été (*m.*)	*summer*
faire	*to do; to make*
il fait frais	*it is cool*
il fait froid	*it is cold*
la fleur	*flower*
en fleurs	*in bloom*
froid	*cold*
l'hirondelle (*f.*)	*swallow (bird)*
l'hiver (*m.*)	*winter*
magnifique	*magnificent, splendid, superb*
marcher	*to walk*
le marronnier	*chestnut tree*
le matin	*morning*
nager	*to swim*
neiger	*to snow*
non	*no*
ou	*or*
un peu	*a little*
la plage	*beach*
il pleut	*it rains; it's raining*
pleuvoir	*to rain*
pour	*for; to*
le printemps	*spring (season)*
le ski	*ski; skiing*
le soir	*evening*
souvent	*often*
sur	*on; upon*
le temps	*weather; time*
le voyage	*trip, journey*

Jamais

Chanter

◄ **2.18** ►

Compréhension et expressions

Les saisons · *Seasons*

In the dialogue, Mr. Jones says, **Nous sommes au printemps** ("We are in spring/It's springtime"). Jeremy states, **J'aime le printemps mais j'adore l'été** ("I like spring, but I love summer"). A little later he says **J'adore le ski en hiver et la bicyclette en automne** ("I love skiing in winter and cycling in the fall").

Here are the seasons (**les saisons**).

le printemps	*spring*
l'été (*m.*)	*summer*
l'automne (*m.*)	*fall*
l'hiver (*m.*)	*winter*

Au printemps, j'admire la nature.	*In the spring, I admire nature.*
En été, j'aime nager dans la mer.	*In summer, I like to swim in the sea.*
En automne, j'aime regarder la télé.	*In autumn, I like to watch TV.*
En hiver, j'aime skier.	*In winter, I like to ski.*

Time of day

le matin	*in the morning*
l'après-midi (*m.*)	*in the afternoon*
le soir	*in the evening*
la nuit	*at night*

Talking about the weather in Paris, Jennifer says:

Le matin et le soir il fait un peu frais.	*In the morning and in the evening, it is a little cool.*

Notice that "in" is not translated in French.

L'après-midi je regarde la télévision et la nuit je rêve.	*In the afternoon I watch TV, and at night I dream.*

translate "En" for in a season but do not translate in or "En" for time of day

Quel temps fait-il? · *What's the weather like?*

It is springtime in France and our friends are wondering **Quel temps fait-il?** The irregular verb **faire** ("to do," "to make") is used to express weather conditions, as when Jennifer says:

> Le matin et le soir, *In the morning and evening,*
> **il fait** frais à Paris. *it is cool in Paris.*

When we say in English "it is cool," in French we say "it makes (does) cool": **il fait frais.**

Le temps · *The weather*
Expressions with *faire*

Il fait chaud.	*It is warm.*
Il fait froid.	*It is cold.*
Il fait frais.	*It is cool.*
Il fait beau.	*It is nice (out).*
Il fait mauvais.	*It is bad (weather):*
Il fait du vent.	*It is windy.*

Autres expressions

Il neige.	*It snows., It is snowing.*
Il pleut.	*It rains., It is raining.*

Il y a ("there is," "there are") can also be used to describe the weather.

Il y a du verglas sur la route.	*There is ice on the road.*
Il y a un orage.	*There is a storm.*
Il y a du brouillard.	*There is fog.*
Il y a de la brume.	*There is mist.*

◄ **2.19** ►
Audio exercise

Everybody talks about the weather. Look at the weather conditions in different cities in the pictures below, and answer the questions on the recording.

EXAMPLE

PROMPT   Quel temps fait-il à Bruxelles?
RESPONSE   Il pleut.

1. Cannes

2. Chicago

3. Annecy
   (French Alps)

4. Lille

5. Strasbourg

6. Brest

◄ **2.20** ►
Structure grammaticale

Qu'est-ce que tu aimes faire? · *What do you like to do?*

Jeremy says J'aime *nager,* **marcher** sur le sable et *jouer* **au basket**
("I like to swim, walk on the sand, and play basketball").

When two verbs follow one another, in French as in English, the
second one takes the infinitive form.

◄ **2.21** ►
Audio exercise

The speaker will ask you what you like to do at different times of
the day or in different seasons and will prompt you in English.
Give the answer in French, then repeat the correct answer after
the speaker.

EXAMPLE

PROMPT   Qu'est-ce que vous aimez faire le matin? (I like to walk.)
RESPONSE   Le matin, j'aime marcher.

◄ **2.22** ►
Exercise

Translate the following sentences into French.

1. *We like to walk on the sand.*

   nous aimons marcher sur le sable

2. *It is windy in Strasbourg.*

   il fait du vent à strashourg ✓

3. *She likes to swim in the sea.*

   Elle aime nager dans la mer

4. *In winter Catherine and André like to ski.*

   L'hiver, Catherine et Andre aiment ~~te ski~~ faire du ski

5. *In the morning it rains in Brest.*

   Le matin, il pleut à Brest

6. *Martine works at night.*

   Martine travaille la nuit

7. *Mr. and Mrs. Dupont like to travel in summer.*

Monsieur Madame Dupont aimon̄t Voyager en l'été.

8. *In winter it snows in Lyon.*

On mege à Lyon en l'hiver.

◄ 2.23 ►
Common pitfalls

Listen on the recording to a class conversation between a student and the teacher. The student is confused by the different uses of the verb **marcher**. Note that the English equivalent of the verb **travailler** ("to work") can only be used with people.

◄ 2.24 ►
Let's take a plunge!

Using what you have learned in this chapter, take the part of one of the speakers in a spontaneous conversation on the recording. You will greet someone and say whether you speak French, where you live and work, what sports you like, what you like to do at different times of the year, and what the weather is like in winter.

◄ 2.25 ►
Vive la différence!

The French-speaking world

French is the spoken language of many countries in the world, not just France. It is the official language of several European countries—Belgium, Switzerland, Luxembourg, and Monaco—as well as many parts of North and West Africa, Southeast Asia, and even in the Pacific—in Tahiti and other Polynesian islands. It is also spoken in parts of the Caribbean and finally, of course, in Quebec, Canada.

French is also one of the six official languages of the United Nations, as well as of the International Postal Union. Along with English, French is an official language of the Olympic Games.

Les Français

The French treasure their privacy and individualism. They do not like to be just one in a crowd. This may help to explain the brick walls and iron railings that surround their houses, as well as their reputed coldness to strangers. It is said that if ten Frenchmen meet in a café to discuss politics, one of their favorite pastimes, ten different points of view will be vociferously expressed.

Foreigners find it difficult to understand how, on the one hand, the French are apt to greet each other with kisses on the cheek, and on the other, they will rarely invite someone into their homes for a meal on the spur of the moment. The reason for this is that the French feel they cannot pay sufficient honor to a guest on short notice, but once earned, their Gallic friendship proves to be deep and lasting.

◄ 2.26 ►
How to make it sound French

The French alphabet has six vowels (**a, e, i, o, u**, and, unlike English, **y**); the other letters of the alphabet are consonants.

A **liaison** is the linking of two words when the first ends in a consonant and the second begins with a vowel or silent **h**. The sound of the two words is run together to produce a smooth effect, as though the terminal consonant of the first word belongs to the second word.

vous_êtes	/vu-zait/
Comment vous_appelez-vous?	/komon vu-za-p-lai-vu/
deux_heures	/da-zur/

Notice that **s** and **x** are pronounced /z/ in a **liaison**.

> Comment_allez vous?
> un grand_hôtel
> c'est_ici

Notice that **d** and **t** are pronounced /t/, but the **t** of the conjunction **et** ("and") is always silent. On the other hand, the **t** of the third-person singular of the verb **être** ("to be"), **est**, is sounded. So be careful when pronouncing **un homme** *et* **une femme** ("a man and a woman"). The **t** is not sounded here. If it were sounded, it would mean **un homme** *est* **une femme** ("a man *is* a woman").

◄ **3** ►

Parlons vacances!

Let's talk about vacation!

OBJECTIVE

In this chapter, you will learn to be straightforward, to express what you have or do not have, and how you feel. To keep up with reality, you'll learn to count. The clock is ticking! You seem to be surrounded by so many different people: find out their nationalities and something about their personalities. You'll also meet that strange character named Astérix.

◄ 3.1 ►

DIALOGUE 1
Oh là là, elle est pressée! · *My, she's in a hurry!*

Our friends are now thinking of their vacation.

Nos trois amis pensent aux vacances.

M. JONES	Vous avez des vacances?
JEREMY	J'ai neuf jours de vacances. Et toi, Jennifer?
JENNIFER	Je ne suis pas sûre... huit, neuf ou dix. Mais quelle heure est-il?
JEREMY	Il est trois heures.
JENNIFER	Oh, là là, je suis en retard. J'ai rendez-vous à quatre heures. Salut les amis.
M. JONES ET JEREMY	Salut, à demain.

◄ 3.2 ►

Petit lexique

avoir rendez-vous	*to have an appointment/a date*
le bois	*wood, woods, grove*
la cerise	*cherry*
cueillir	*to pick, to gather*
à demain	*see you tomorrow*
être en retard	*to be late*
être pressé(e)	*to be in a hurry*
être sûr(e)	*to be sure, to be certain*
l'heure (*f.*)	*hour, time*
le jour	*day*
mais	*but*
neuf	*new*
le panier	*basket*
Quelle heure est-il?	*What time is it?*
seront	*will be*
toutes rouges	*all red*
les vacances (*f.pl.*)	*vacation*

◄ 3.3 ►
Compréhension et expressions

Comptons! · *Let's count!*

0   zéro
1   un
2   deux ("x" pronounced /z/ before a vowel)
3   trois
4   quatre
5   cinq
6   six ("x" pronounced /z/ before a vowel)
7   sept
8   huit ("t" pronounced before a vowel)
9   neuf
10 dix ("x" pronounced /z/ before a vowel)
11 onze
12 douze

Notice that the **-f** of **neuf** is pronounced /v/ before **heures** ("hours") and **ans** ("years").

◄ 3.4 ►
Audio practice

You will now hear the numbers sung from one to twelve (**un à douze**) to the tune of "Frère Jacques." Listen, and then sing during the pause on the recording.

◄ 3.5 ►
Audio practice

Now, listen to the song that gives the numbers by threes.

Chanson

Un deux trois, nous irons au bois.
Quatre cinq six, cueillir des cerises.
Sept huit neuf, dans un panier neuf.
Dix onze douze, elles seront toutes rouges.

One two three, we will go to the wood.
Four five six, harvest the cherries.
Seven eight nine, in a new basket.
Ten eleven twelve, they will all be red.

◄ **3.6** ►

Compréhension et expressions

Telling time

> Quelle heure est-il?   *What time is it?*

Il est + the hour is used to tell time.

> Il est deux heures.   *It is two o'clock.*

Quelle heure est-il?

> Il est trois heures.   *It is three o'clock.*
> Il est cinq heures.   *It is five o'clock.*
> Il est dix heures.   *It is ten o'clock.*
> Il est six heures.   *It is six o'clock.*

 ◄ **3.7** ►

Audio exercise

Listen to the number of chimes on the recording, then say aloud what time it is.

EXAMPLE

PROMPT   Quelle heure est-il? (two chimes)
RESPONSE   Il est deux heures.   *It is two o'clock.*

◄ **3.8** ►

Structure grammaticale

avoir · *to have*

In the dialogue Jeremy says **J'ai neuf jours de vacances,** meaning "I have nine days of vacation." Jeremy is using the verb **avoir** ("to have").

> **J'ai** la cassette de français.   *I have the French cassette.*
> Tu **as** les livres de français.   *You have the French books.*
> Il **a** les chocolats et les   *He has the chocolates and the*
>   bonbons.   *candies.*
> Elle **a** les croissants.   *She has the croissants.*
> On **a** la réservation.   *We have the reservation.*
> Nous **avons** le café.   *We have the coffee.*
> Vous **avez** le plan du métro.   *You have the subway map.*
> Ils/Elles **ont** le numéro   *They have the phone number.*
>   de téléphone.

◄ 3.9 ►
Audio exercise

The speaker will give you the time of day. Tell the cabdriver you have an appointment an hour later. You will use the phrase **J'ai rendez-vous à...** "I have a meeting at . . ."

EXAMPLE

PROMPT   Il est huit heures.
RESPONSE   J'ai rendez-vous à neuf heures.

◄ 3.10 ►
Audio exercise

Listen to the question. Answer affirmatively, and repeat the correct answer after the speaker.

EXAMPLE

PROMPT   Vous avez le livre?
RESPONSE   Oui, j'ai le livre.

◄ 3.11 ►
Exercise

Complete the following sentences with the correct form of **avoir**.

1. Jeremy ___*a*___ deux amis français, il ___*a*___ aussi trois amis américains.

2. Ils ___*ont*___ la possibilité de voyager en Concorde.

3. Nous ___*avons*___ la carte de crédit dans le sac. (le sac, *the bag*)

4. Gisèle ___*a*___ un panier de cerises rouges.

5. Vous ___*avez*___ une réservation pour le concert?

6. J'___*ai*___ quatre euros et toi tu ___*as*___ six euros. Nous ___*avons*___ dix euros au total.

7. On ___*a*___ rendez-vous chez le dentiste à quatre heures.

8. Elle ___*a*___ un poste de réceptionniste au musée du Louvre. (un poste, *a position/job*)

◄ **3.12** ►
Structure grammaticale
Sensation et condition

To express state of being, condition, or feeling, in French as in English, use the verb **être** ("to be").

Je **suis** malade.	*I am sick.*
Je **suis** fatigué.	*I am tired.*
Je **suis** heureux.	*I am happy.*
Il **est** en retard.	*He is late.*
Elle **est** en avance.	*She is early.*
Nous **sommes** à l'heure.	*We are on time.*

However, to express certain sensations in French, we use the verb **avoir** ("to have").

J'**ai** faim.	*I am hungry.*
Il **a** soif.	*He is thirsty.*
Tu **as** chaud.	*You are warm.*
Ils **ont** froid.	*They are cold.*
Elle **a** sommeil.	*She is sleepy.*
Nous **avons** peur.	*We are afraid.*
Vous **avez** de la chance.	*You are lucky.*

Age

We also use **avoir** to indicate the age of a person.

Tu as quel âge?,	*How old are you?*
Quel âge as-tu?	
J'ai dix ans.	*I am ten. (literally, I have ten years.)*

 ◄ **3.13** ►
Audio exercise

The speaker will prompt you in English to express certain conditions or sensations. Listen carefully, and respond in French, then repeat the correct response after the speaker.

EXAMPLE

PROMPT   She is lucky.
RESPONSE   Elle a de la chance.

◄ 3.14 ►
Structure grammaticale

La forme négative · *The negative form*

To form the negative of a verb, place the particle **ne** before the verb and **pas** after it. If the verb starts with a vowel or silent **h**, **ne** becomes **n'**.

> Je suis français.
> Je **ne** suis **pas** américain.
>
> Il est six heures, le concert est à neuf heures.
> Nous **ne** sommes **pas** pressés.
>
> J'ai le livre.
> Je **n'**ai **pas** la cassette.
>
> J'habite à Paris.
> Je **n'**habite **pas** à New York.

◄ 3.15 ►
Exercise

Answer the following questions in the negative.

EXAMPLE   Vous habitez à Paris?

Non, je n'habite pas à Paris.

1. Tu parles anglais?

   non, tu ne parle pas anglais

2. Elle travaille à l'aéroport?

   Elle ne travaille pas à l'

3. Ils ont soif?

   Ils n'ont pas soif

4. Nous avons faim?

   Nous n'avons pas faim

5. On aime le football?

   On n'aime pas

6. Tu as sommeil?

   tu n'as pas

◄ **3.16** ►
DIALOGUE 2
Jennifer

Jennifer was late for her four o'clock appointment. She has left her two friends, Jeremy and Mr. Jones, who are now carrying on the conversation. Let's listen to them.

Jennifer est partie. Jeremy et M. Jones continuent la conversation. Écoutons-les!

M. JONES	Neuf jours de vacances, c'est court!
JEREMY	L'année prochaine, j'ai de grandes vacances et Jennifer aussi.
M. JONES	Jennifer est toujours pressée. C'est une fille active, chaleureuse...
JEREMY	Et très intelligente! J'aime les personnes qui ont l'esprit rapide.
M. JONES	Et les cheveux longs et blonds!

◄ **3.17** ►
Petit lexique

actif(-ive)	*active*
l'année (*f.*)	*year*
blond(e)	*blond*
chaleureux(-euse)	*warm, warm-hearted*
les cheveux (*m.pl.*)	*hair*
l'esprit (*m.*)	*spirit; mind*
grand(e)	*big, tall*
haut(e)	*high*
intelligent(e)	*intelligent*
long(ue)	*long*
la personne	*person*
prochain(e)	*next*
qui	*who, that, which*
rapide	*fast*

◄ **3.18** ►
Compréhension et expressions

la personne · *person*

The French word **personne** ("person") is always feminine, even when it applies to a man.

M. Jones est **une** personne intelligente.	*Mr. Jones is an intelligent person.*
Le président français est **une** personne importante.	*The French president is an important person.*

l'esprit · *mind*

The word **esprit** means "mind," "spirit," or "wit" in French.

Les Français ont l'esprit critique.	*The French have a critical mind.*
Les mauvais esprits arrivent le soir de Halloween.	*Bad spirits come out on Halloween.*
Elle a de l'esprit.	*She is witty.*

les cheveux · *hair*

Jennifer a les **cheveux blonds**. The word **cheveux** is always plural in French when speaking of a person's hair.

Les cheveux de Joséphine **sont** courts.	*Josephine's hair is short.*

c'est · *it is*

You noticed in the dialogue the expression **c'est court**. When an adjective is used with **c'est**, the adjective remains in its masculine form.

La France, c'est **grand**.
La tour Eiffel, c'est **haut**.
La mousse au chocolat, c'est **bon**.

◄ **3.19** ►
Structure grammaticale
Les adjectifs · *Adjectives*

In the dialogue, Jeremy says **L'année prochaine j'ai de grandes vacances.** Here, **grandes** is the feminine plural form of the adjective **grand**.

In French, adjectives agree in gender and number with the noun (or pronoun) they modify. Therefore, **grandes** takes an **-e** to mark its feminine gender and an **-s** to express the plural. Most regular adjectives form their plural this way.

Pierre est grand et Marie est grande aussi: ils sont grands.	*Pierre is tall and Marie is also tall: they are tall.*
Florence est petite et Delphine est petite aussi: elles sont petites.	*Florence is small and Delphine is also small: they are small.*

Adjectifs réguliers · *Regular adjectives*

Look at the following regular adjectives.

MASCULINE	FEMININE	
charmant	charmante	*charming*
content	contente	*happy, content*
court	courte	*short*
droit	droite	*straight*
indépendant	indépendante	*independent*
intéressant	intéressante	*interesting*
lourd	lourde	*heavy*
petit	petite	*small*
prochain	prochaine	*next*
prudent	prudente	*cautious*
vert	verte	*green*

If the last syllable of a masculine adjective ends in **-d, -n, -s,** or **-t**, the final consonant is pronounced in the feminine forms.

La robe est verte /vert/.
Les Françaises /-saiz/ sont indépendantes /-dant/.

Adjectifs irréguliers · *Irregular adjectives*

Adjectives ending in silent -**e** in the masculine singular do not change in the feminine singular.

MASCULINE	FEMININE	
aimable	aimable	*kind*
alerte	alerte	*alert*
calme	calme	*calm*
égoïste	égoïste	*selfish*
idéaliste	idéaliste	*idealistic*
jaune	jaune	*yellow*
moderne	moderne	*modern*
optimiste	optimiste	*optimistic*
rapide	rapide	*fast*
rouge	rouge	*red*
sociable	sociable	*sociable*

Adjectives ending in -**f** in the masculine singular form their feminine in -**ve**.

MASCULINE	FEMININE	
actif	acti**ve**	*active*
agressif	agressi**ve**	*aggressive*
attentif	attenti**ve**	*attentive*
émotif	émoti**ve**	*emotional*
impulsif	impulsi**ve**	*impulsive*
positif	positi**ve**	*positive*

Les étudiants ont l'esprit positif; ils sont calmes et attentifs.	*The students are in a positive frame of mind; they are calm and attentive.*
Les étudiantes ont l'esprit positif; elles sont calmes et attentives.	*The students are in a positive frame of mind; they are calm and attentive.*

◀ 3.20 ▶
Audio practice: Adjective endings that are pronounced

On the recording, try to hear the difference in pronunciation between the last syllable of the adjectives (for example, **américain** and **a-mé-ri-cai-ne**), and repeat after the speaker.

1. Jeremy est américain.   Jennifer est américai**ne**.
2. Moussa et Fatimata sont   Fatimata et Aichatou sont africai**nes**.
   africains.
3. Pierre est français.   Isabelle est françai**se**.
4. John est anglais.   Connie est anglai**se**.
5. Pierre est blond.   Marie est blon**de**.
6. Il est intelligent.   Elle est intelligen**te**.

◀ 3.21 ▶
Audio exercise

Answer the question with the same adjective in its appropriate form and add **aussi** ("also"). Then, repeat the correct answer after the speaker.

EXAMPLE

PROMPT   Pierre est charmant, et Marie?
RESPONSE   Marie est charmante aussi.

◀ 3.22 ▶
Exercise

Complete the following sentences with the appropriate form (masculine or feminine, singular or plural) of the adjective.

italien	espagnol	anglaise
japonais	canadienne	cubain
français	mexicaine	
américains	chinois	

1. La princesse Diana est _anglaise_.
2. L'empereur Hirohito est _japonais_.
3. Céline Dion est _canadienne_.
4. Charles de Gaulle et Édith Piaf sont
   français.

5. Léonard de Vinci est _Halyen_.
6. Mao Tsé Tung est _Chinois_.
7. George Washington et Abraham Lincoln sont
   americans.
8. Salvador Dali est _Espanole_.
9. Fidel Castro est _Cubain_.
10. La tortilla est _Mexicaine_

◄ 3.23 ►
DIALOGUE 3
Astérix

A little later Jennifer returns to her friends. She notices they are concentrating deeply on their reading. She is puzzled when she sees the book *Astérix le Gaulois*.

Un peu plus tard, Jennifer est de retour avec ses amis. Elle remarque qu'ils se concentrent sur leur lecture. Elle est perplexe en voyant le titre du livre: Astérix le Gaulois.

JENNIFER   Qu'est-ce que c'est?

JEREMY   C'est l'étude psychanalytique des Français avec Astérix.

JENNIFER   Tu es malade ou tu es fou?

JEREMY   Je suis en pleine forme.

JENNIFER   Alors, qui est Astérix?

M. JONES   Le héros d'une bande dessinée française. C'est un homme avec des moustaches énormes. Il est petit, blond, musclé et très fort.

JEREMY   Il représente assez bien l'esprit français. Il est intelligent, aventureux, astucieux et très indépendant.

M. JONES   Quelquefois, il est aussi vaniteux, impatient, agressif et irritable... comme les Français!

◄ 3.24 ►
Petit lexique

agressif(-ve)   *aggressive*
assez   *enough, sufficiently*
astucieux(-euse)   *astute, resourceful*
aventureux(-euse)   *adventurous*

la bande dessinée	*cartoon, comic strip or book*
comme	*as, like*
énorme	*huge*
être en pleine forme	*to feel great*
l'étude (*f.*)	*study (of a subject)*
fort(e)	*strong*
fou/folle	*mad, crazy*
le héros	*hero*
l'homme (*m.*)	*man*
impatient(e)	*impatient, eager*
indépendant(e)	*independent*
irritable	*irritable*
malade	*sick*
la moustache	*mustache*
musclé(e)	*muscular*
psychanalytique	*psychoanalytic*
quelquefois	*sometimes*
Qu'est-ce que c'est?	*What is it?*
représenter	*to represent*
vaniteux(-euse)	*vain*

◄ 3.25 ►
Compréhension et expressions

Qu'est-ce que c'est? · *What is it?*

When she sees the book Jeremy and Mr. Jones are reading, Jennifer is surprised and asks, **Qu'est-ce que c'est?** ("What is it?"). When using **Qu'est-ce que c'est?**, the answer will be a *thing*.

Qu'est-ce que c'est le plat du jour?	*What is the daily special?*
C'est du homard à l'armoricaine.	*It is lobster in Armoric-style sauce.*

Qui est-ce?, Qui c'est?, Qui est-ce que c'est? · *Who is he/she?*

In the dialogue, Jennifer asks **Qui est Astérix?** ("Who is Astérix?"). When using **Qui?**, the answer will be a *person*.

Qui est-ce?	*Who is he?*
C'est Astérix. Ce n'est pas une personne réelle.	*He's Astérix. He is not a real person.*

en pleine forme · *feeling great, in great shape*

In the dialogue, Jeremy tells Jennifer, **Je suis en pleine forme** ("I am feeling great").

Comment allez-vous?	*How are you?*
Comme ci comme ça; je ne suis pas en pleine forme.	*So-so; I am not feeling great.*

◄ 3.26 ►
Structure grammaticale

D'autres adjectifs irréguliers · *More irregular adjectives*

Adjectives ending in **-eux** form their feminine in **-euse**. Many of these adjectives correspond to adjectives ending in "-ous" in English.

MASCULINE	FEMININE	
ambitieux	ambitieuse	*ambitious*
aventureux	aventureuse	*adventurous*
courageux	courageuse	*courageous*
dangereux	dangereuse	*dangerous*
délicieux	délicieuse	*delicious*
furieux	furieuse	*furious*
généreux	généreuse	*generous*

La mousse au chocolat: c'est délicieux.	*That chocolate mousse is delicious.*
Jennifer est chaleureuse.	*Jennifer is warm (a warm-hearted person).*

NOTE: If the masculine singular form of the adjective ends in **-s** or **-x**, the masculine plural does not change.

le livre anglais	**les** livres anglais
L'homme est généreux.	**Les** hommes sont généreux.

Here are a few more adjectives ending in **-eux**.

MASCULINE	FEMININE	
amoureux	amoureuse	*in love*
heureux	heureuse	*happy*
malheureux	malheureuse	*unhappy*

◄ **3.27** ►
Exercise

Complete the following sentences with the correct form of the adjective in parentheses.

1. Jeremy est __grand__. (grand)
2. Le thé est __vert__. (vert)
3. Delphine a les cheveux __blonds__. (blond)
4. Francine n'est pas __amoureuse__ (amoureux)
5. Jennifer est __chaleureuse__. (chaleureux)
6. Elle est __fatiguée__ et __irritable__.
   (fatigué, irritable)
7. Elles sont __sincères__ mais très __timides__.
   (sincère, timide)
8. Marie a des problèmes; elle est __impulsive__.
   (impulsif)

◄ **3.28** ►
Common pitfalls

Listen to the following class interaction between the student and the teacher on the recording as the student tries to explain that he is hungry.

This interaction shows us the pitfalls that exist in any foreign language if we try to speak with the patterns of our own native tongue. No language can be exactly translated into another. Therefore, it is essential not to try to translate expressions literally. There is no explanation for why French and English differ in expressing the same concepts. But in this case we can say that biological needs, desires, and sensations are used with the verb **avoir** ("to have"), for example, **avoir faim**, **avoir soif**, **avoir froid**, **avoir chaud**.

◄ 3.29 ►
Let's take a plunge!

Using what you have learned in this chapter, answer the speaker in a spontaneous conversation about how you feel.

◄ 3.30 ►
Vive la différence!

The French have developed the art of nonverbal communication almost as much as the Italians. In one simultaneous action, the Frenchman curls his mouth, pouts his lips, raises his shoulders, turns his palms toward the sky, and says **Oh là là!**

Les vacances

French workers are generally given five weeks of paid annual vacation, most of which they take all at once. For the French, **les vacances** is a sacred and very important part of life and living.

Despite repeated efforts by the French government over the years to encourage workers to stagger the dates of their vacations, many firms, factories, restaurants, theaters, and the like close during the months of July and August, thus giving people exactly the same vacation period.

Imagine the gridlock as vacationers hit the main roads out of Paris and other large cities and head for the beaches. Imagine, too, the frustration of the unknowing foreign visitors who arrive in France at that time, only to find many of the city attractions they had planned to visit now in gravelike stillness!

◄ 3.31 ►
How to make it sound French

FRENCH LETTER	EXAMPLE WORDS	NEAREST ENGLISH SOUND
r	retard, rendez-vous	like a brief gargle
j	bonjour, je	like "s" in "pleasure"

Some French sounds never occur in English. Consequently, the best way for English speakers to reproduce these sounds is by listening to French people speak and trying to imitate them. The following may be of some help, though.

The French **u** sound, as in **salut**, is one of the hardest sounds for the Anglo-Saxon tongue. This sound is produced by puckering the lips forward into an o shape (rather like a chimpanzee making its happy hoot sound, "ou-ou"), and at the same time pressing the back edges of the tongue, curled from side to side, against the upper molar teeth.

◄ 3.32 ►
Activities

To mark the completion of chapters 1 through 3, try the following activities.

A. Here are various situations. What would you say in each one of them?

1. How do you greet a close friend when you meet him or her?
   Cou   bonjour   . Ca va ?

2. How would you greet a less familiar person (using a more formal greeting)? _Bonjour   Comment allez vous_

3. What do you say when you are leaving?
   Au revin

4. Someone gives you something. What do you say?
   merci

5. You are going to bed. What do you say?
   Bone nuit

6. You meet Jennifer in the street; greet her!
   Bonjour Madmoiselly

7. You meet M. and Mme Delapierre; greet them!
   Bonjour monsieur et madame

8. You answer the phone; what do you say?
   Bonjour ? Il

B. Here are some common expressions. Choose the right one to fit the situations below.

Bonne chance! ("Good luck!")
Joyeux anniversaire! ("Happy birthday!")
Excusez-moi! ("Sorry!")
Au secours. ("Help.")
Je suis en retard/en avance. ("I am late/early.")

1. C'est l'anniversaire de Jennifer. Qu'est-ce que vous dites?
   Joyeux anniversaire!

2. Vous avez rendez-vous à dix heures; vous arrivez à onze heures. Qu'est-ce que vous dites?
   Excusez-moi Je suis en retard.

3. Jeremy prépare un examen. Qu'est-ce que vous dites?
   Bonne Chance!

4. Vous êtes en danger. Qu'est-ce que vous dites?
   Au secours

5. Vous poussez une personne dans le bus. Qu'est-ce que vous dites? *Excuse-moi* (poussez, *to push*)

C. Qui est-ce? Qu'est-ce que c'est? Read these short descriptions and guess who or what is being described.

1. Il n'est pas réel mais il a un succès phénoménal. Il habite en Gaule et voyage beaucoup, en Belgique, en Italie, en Égypte. Il représente assez bien l'esprit français.
   Qui est-ce? *Cette Droit*

2. C'est une attraction touristique. Elle a deux nationalités: américaine et canadienne. Elle a une force exceptionnelle . et elle est dangereuse. Les touristes admirent sa beauté... Attention, quelquefois elle est furieuse.
   Qu'est que c'est? *Cetua Braque Niagara falls*

3. C'est un grand homme français du dix-neuvième siècle. Il est petit, courageux et très ambitieux. Il est aussi souvent amoureux. Il gouverne la France et une partie de l'Europe. Les Anglais sont ses ennemis mortels. (le siècle, *century*)
   Qui est-ce? *Napoleon*

4. Ce n'est pas une personne. Elle est Française d'origine mais elle habite à New York dans une petite île. Elle représente l'amitié entre la France et les États-Unis. (l'île (*f.*), *island;* l'amitié (*f.*), *friendship*)

   Qu'est-ce que c'est? _____ Statue of liberty

5. Ce n'est pas une personne. Elle a la nationalité italienne mais elle habite à Paris dans un musée. Elle est le symbole de la jeunesse et elle a un sourire mystérieux. (le sourire, *smile*)

   Qu'est-ce que c'est? _____ Mona lisa _____

◄ **4** ►

Les trois «J» à Paris
The three "J"s in Paris

OBJECTIVE

In this chapter, you arrive in Paris and decide to take a taxi. Most importantly, you need to be able to deal with cabdrivers and tell them clearly where you want to go! Be polite, but assertive! Perhaps you want to enjoy a nice drink on the terrace of a French café? Don't relax too much, however; keep track of time, and get familiar with the new currency, the euro.

◄ **4.1** ►
DIALOGUE 1
Taxi!

Our friends are at Charles de Gaulle airport. They decide to take a taxi to go to the Café des Deux Magots on the trendy Rive Gauche. Let's follow them!

Nos amis sont à l'aéroport Charles de Gaulle; ils décident de pren-dre un taxi pour aller au café des Deux Magots. Suivons-les et écou-tons leur conversation!

JEREMY	Taxi, taxi!
CHAUFFEUR	C'est pour où?
JENNIFER	Nous voudrions aller Rive Gauche, dans un café très parisien.
CHAUFFEUR	Alors, vous avez le Procope, le Flore ou les Deux Magots, le café préféré de Hemingway et de Jean-Paul Sartre.
M. JONES, JEREMY ET JENNIFER	Aux Deux Magots, s'il vous plaît!
CHAUFFEUR	Alors, montez et allons-y pour les Deux Magots.

◄ **4.2** ►
Petit lexique

aller	*to go*
allons-y	*let's go (there)*
C'est pour où?	*Where to?*
monter	*to get in, to go up*
où	*where*
parisien(ne)	*Parisian*
préféré(e)	*preferred, favorite*
s'il vous plaît/s'il te plaît	*please*
le taxi	*taxi*
je voudrais (vouloir)	*I would like*
nous voudrions	*we would like*

◄ **4.3** ►

Compréhension et expressions

C'est pour où? · *Where to?*

Taxi drivers can be quite informal and will ask you as soon as you board their cab, **C'est pour où?** or **On va où?**, which literally mean "Where to?" or "Where are we going?" A more formal way to address the passenger would be **Vous désirez aller?**

Allons-y pour... · *Let's go to/Why don't we go to . . .*

This is an informal way to say "Let's go to . . ."

Allons-y pour l'aéroport Charles de Gaulle.	*Let's go to Charles de Gaulle airport!*
Allons-y pour le jardin du Luxembourg.	*Why don't we go to the Luxembourg garden!*

Je voudrais... · *I would like . . .*

A polite way to express what you want is to use **Je voudrais** ("I would like"). This is followed by the infinitive form of the verb that expresses the action you want to accomplish.

Je voudrais aller...	*I would like to go . . .*
Je voudrais aller au musée du Louvre.	*I would like to go to the Louvre Museum.*
Je voudrais aller à la tour Eiffel.	*I would like to go to the Eiffel Tower.*
Je voudrais aller à la tour Montparnasse.	*I would like to go to the Montparnasse Tower.*
Je voudrais aller à l'hôtel Intercontinental.	*I would like to go to the Intercontinental Hotel.*

Je voudrais can also be followed by a noun. In this case it becomes a request rather than a wish and should be followed by one of the following expressions:

s'il te plaît ("if you please") when you are talking to one person you are familiar with

OR

s'il vous plaît when you are being formal or talking to more than one person

Je voudrais un pepsi, s'il vous plaît.	*I would like a Pepsi, please.*

◄ **4.4** ►
Audio exercise

You are in Paris. Using the prompt on the recording, tell the different places you would like to go to. Then, repeat the correct response after the speaker.

EXAMPLE

PROMPT   Au quartier Latin.

RESPONSE   Je voudrais aller au quartier Latin.

◄ **4.5** ►
Structure grammaticale

à/à la/au/aux

Je voudrais aller **au** musée
du Louvre, **à la** tour Eiffel,
à l'hôtel de France et **aux**
Champs-Élysées.

I would like to go to the Louvre
Museum, to the Eiffel Tower,
to the Hôtel de France, and
to the Champs-Élysées.

Notice that **à** is used here with a definite article: **le**, **la**, **l'**, or **les**. In such cases it combines or contracts with the article to form:

à + le → **au** (*masculine*)
à + la → **à la** (*feminine*)

If the noun is singular and starts with a vowel or silent **h**, it becomes: **à l'**.

à + les → **aux** (*plural*)

NOTE: Contraction occurs with the masculine singular and plural forms.

Les amis voudraient une
glace **au** chocolat.
un sorbet **au** cassis
une glace à la vanille
un café **au** lait
une tarte **aux** pommes

The friends would like a
chocolate ice cream.
a blackcurrant sherbet
a vanilla ice cream
a coffee with milk
an apple pie

◄ **4.6** ►
Audio exercise

Look at the four situations below, representing different places that you want to go by taxi. Listen to the taxi driver on the recording; greet him and tell him your destination. Use the phrase **je voudrais aller**.

EXAMPLE

PROMPT   Bonjour, vous désirez aller?

RESPONSE   Bonjour Monsieur, je voudrais aller à la gare Montparnasse.

1. la tour Eiffel

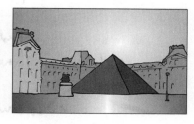

2. le musée du Louvre

3. l'arc de Triomphe

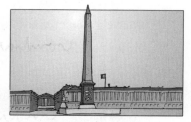

4. la place de la Concorde

◄ **4.7** ►
Exercise

Complete the exercise that follows, using **je voudrais** and **s'il te plaît** or **s'il vous plaît**.

EXAMPLE   (Marie-Paule and Marc are friends.)

Marie-Paule: Tu désires une orange ou une banane?

Marc: Je __voudrais__ une orange, __s'il te plaît__.

1. Le garçon: Vous désirez un thé ou un café?

    Jeremy: Je __voudrais__ un thé,

    __s'il vous plaît__.

2. Le garçon: Vous désirez un pepsi ou un coca-cola?

    M. Jones: Je __voudrais__ un coca-cola,

    __s'il vous plaît__.

3. (Julie, to her friend)

    Julie: Je __voudrais__ le livre de français,

    __s'il vous plaît__

4. (Julie, Marie-Paule, Marc)

    Marie-Paule et Marc: Vous désirez?

    Julie: Je __voudrais__ aller au cinéma avec vous,

    _____.

5. (Antoine and his mother)

    Antoine: Je __voudrais__ aller à la tour Eiffel,

    _____, Maman.

◄ **4.8** ►
Exercise

Complete the following sentences with **au**, **à la**, **à l'**, or **aux**.

1. Nous allons __aux__ Champs-Élysées.

2. Je suis __au__ quartier Latin.

3. Pierre et Julie sont __à la__ bibliothèque. (la bibliothèque, *library*)

4. Nos amis sont _qux_ Deux Magots.

5. Ils désirent un thé _au_ citron.

6. Jeremy mange une pizza _à la_ tomate. (la tomate, *tomato*)

7. Jennifer commande un sandwich _au_ jambon. (le jambon, *ham*)

8. Il mange des spaghettis _à la_ sauce tomate. (la sauce tomate, *tomato sauce*)

9. Nous commandons des glaces _à la_ vanille.

10. Nous voudrions aller _à l'_ hôtel.

◄ **4.9** ►

Structure grammaticale

L'impératif · *Imperative*

The taxi driver tells our friends **Montez** ("Get in"). He is using the imperative form of the verb. The imperative is used to give commands and make suggestions.

Generally, the imperative is formed by using the present tense and dropping the subject pronouns **tu**, **vous**, and **nous**.

PRESENT	IMPERATIVE
Tu montes dans le taxi.	**Monte** dans le taxi. *Get in the taxi.*
Vous montez dans le taxi.	**Montez** dans le taxi. *Get in the taxi.*
Nous montons dans le taxi.	**Montons** dans le taxi. *Let's get in the taxi.*

Notice that the **-s** of the familiar **tu** form of **-er** verbs is dropped, and that the imperative form ends in **-e**.

The negative imperative follows the negative pattern of other conjugated verbs: **ne/n'** + verb + **pas**.

N'achetez pas les chocolats.   *Don't buy the chocolates.*
Ne regardons pas la télé.   *Let's not watch TV.*

◄ 4.10 ►
Audio exercise

Listen to the questions on the recording; then, using the impera-tive, politely request that the task be done. Repeat the correct answer after the speaker.

EXAMPLE

PROMPT   Vous ne réservez pas l'hôtel?
RESPONSE   Réservez l'hôtel, s'il vous plaît!

◄ 4.11 ►
Exercise

Translate the following sentences into French.

1. *Paul and Patrick, do not play basketball!*

   _Ne Jouez pas ._____

2. *Let's visit France.*

   _Visitons France_____

3. *Étienne, work in Paris!*

   _traivie à Paris_____

4. *Let's go up the Eiffel Tower.*

   _Montons à la effu_____

5. *Listen to the teacher!*

   _Geoutez le_____

6. *Let's speak French!*

   _Parlons Francais_____

7. *Anne, eat the cake!*

   _mange le gateau_____

8. *Let's look at the phone number.*

   _regardons de nuhu du_____

9. *Françoise, Karine, and Sabrina, visit the Louvre Museum!*

   _Visitez le ~~Lous~~ mussae_____

10. *Laurent, count!*

    _____

◀ 4.12 ▶
DIALOGUE 2
Aux Deux Magots · *At the Deux Magots*

Our friends are sitting on the Deux Magots terrace, and they order some drinks.

Nos amis sont assis à la terrasse du café des Deux Magots et ils commandent des boissons.

LE SERVEUR	Vous désirez, Messieurs-dames?
M. JONES	Commandez d'abord!
JENNIFER	Pour moi, un Perrier-citron, s'il vous plaît, et pour toi Jeremy?
JEREMY	Je prends un thé, merci!
LE SERVEUR	Et pour Monsieur?
JENNIFER	Pour lui, une blonde. Il adore la blonde.
M. JONES	Oui, c'est vrai; une blonde, s'il vous plaît.
LE SERVEUR	Très bien; Mademoiselle prend un Perrier-citron et Messieurs prennent un thé et une blonde.
JENNIFER	D'accord, mais excusez-moi, je voudrais aller aux toilettes.

◀ 4.13 ▶
Petit lexique

la blonde	*pale ale (beer)*
le citron	*lemon*
d'abord	*first*
d'accord	*okay, all right*
désirer	*to want; to wish*
mais	*but*
prendre	*to take*
le serveur	*waiter*
les toilettes (*f.pl.*)	*toilet*
aller aux toilettes	*to go to the bathroom*
vrai(e)	*true*

Extension de vocabulaire

l'apéritif (*m.*)	*aperitif, before-dinner drink*
la bière pression	*draft beer*
la boisson	*drink, beverage*
le café noir	*black coffee*

le café crème	*coffee with milk/cream*
le cassis	*blackcurrant*
l'eau (*f.*)	*water*
l'eau minérale	*mineral water*
plate	*noncarbonated (mineral water)*
gazeuse/pétillante	*carbonated*
l'expresso (*m.*)	*espresso*
la glace	*ice cream; ice*
la fraise	*strawberry*
la framboise	*raspberry*
le jus	*juice*
la menthe	*mint*
l'orange (*f.*)	*orange*
le pamplemousse	*grapefruit*
la poire	*pear*
la pomme	*apple*
l'addition (*f.*)	*check, bill*
la bouteille	*bottle*
la carafe	*carafe, decanter*
la tasse	*cup*
le verre	*glass*

◄ 4.14 ►
Compréhension et expressions

In the dialogue, Mr. Jones tells Jennifer and Jeremy, **Commandez d'abord** ("Order first"). The following three expressions are used to express the sequence of events.

d'abord	*first*
ensuite	*then, next, afterward*
enfin	*finally*

Jennifer knows that Mr. Jones likes **une blonde**, meaning **une bière blonde**, in contrast to **une brune** (**une bière brune**).

une blonde	*pale ale, lager*
une brune	*dark beer, stout beer*

La blonde and **la brune** can also apply to a blond or brunette woman.

◀ 4.15 ▶
Structure grammaticale

Les articles indéfinis · *Indefinite articles*

un/une/des

> Aux Deux Magots, les trois «J» commandent **des** boissons; **un** Perrier-citron, **un** thé et **une** bière.

We have already seen the definite articles **le, la, l', les,** equivalent to "the" in English. We are now going to learn the indefinite articles and the way to say "a," "an," and "some" in French.

un	masculin singulier	un café
		un garçon
		un homme
une	féminin singulier	une eau minérale
		une orange
		une femme
des	masculin et féminin pluriel	des cafés
		des hommes
		des oranges

Verbe irrégulier: *prendre* ("to take")

In the café, Jennifer says . . .

> Je **prends** un Perrier-citron.   *I'll have a lemon Perrier.*

. . . and the waiter says:

> Mademoiselle **prend**... et   *The young lady is having . . .*
> Messieurs **prennent**...   *and the gentlemen are having . . .*

Prends, prend, and **prennent** are three forms of the verb **prendre.**

Notice that **prendre** is used (rather than **avoir**) when ordering food and drinks.

> Je **prends** un jus d'ananas.   *I'll have a pineapple juice.*

Here is the conjugation of **prendre**.

Je **prends** le train.	*I take/am taking the train.*
Tu **prends** une tasse de chocolat.	*You take/are having a cup of chocolate.*
Prend-on un thé nature?	*Do we take/Are we having a plain tea?*
Nous **prenons** un sandwich au fromage.	*We take/are having a cheese sandwich.*
Prenez-vous une crêpe à la saucisse?	*Do you take/Are you having a crêpe with sausage?*
Elles **prennent** des photos.	*They take/are taking (some) pictures.*

The verbs **apprendre** ("to learn") and **comprendre** ("to understand") follow the same pattern as **prendre**.

Les étudiants **apprennent** et **comprennent** le français.	*The students learn and understand French.*

 ◄ **4.16** ►
Audio exercise

You are in a French café. Place your order in French, following the prompts on the recording in English. Then, repeat the correct response after the speaker.

EXAMPLE

PROMPT   I want a Coke, please!

RESPONSE   Je voudrais un coca-cola, s'il vous plaît.

◄ **4.17** ►
Exercise

Complete the following sentences with the correct form of the indefinite article: **un**, **une**, or **des**.

1. _____ café, s'il vous plaît!

2. Vous désirez _____ thé ou _____ eau minérale?

3. Je voudrais _____ fraises avec _____ citron pressé.

4. Tu prends _____ bière pression ou _____ verre de lait?

5. Nous désirons _____ bouteille de champagne.

6. Elle prend _____ crème brûlée.

◄ 4.18 ►
Exercise

Circle the correct article in the following sentences.

1. Je n'aime pas (le / la / les) bière.

2. Je voudrais (un / la / le / une) verre de lait.

3. Nous prenons (un / des / une) thé au citron.

4. Pour moi (la / une / des) eau minérale, s'il vous plaît!

5. J'adore (la / les / un / le) Kir.

◄ 4.19 ►
Exercise

Fill in the blank with the correct form of the verbs **prendre, apprendre**, or **comprendre** and the correct article: **un, une, des**.

Qu'est-ce que vous _____ (prendre)
Messieurs-dames?

Les amis commandent _____ boissons. Jennifer

_____ (prendre) _____ lait–fraise, Jeremy

et M. Jones _____ (prendre) _____ bouteille

d'eau minérale. Le garçon arrive avec _____ bouteille de

champagne. M. Jones explique qu'ils ne désirent pas

_____ bouteille de champagne, mais _____ bouteille d'eau

minérale. Le garçon est furieux et il ne _____

(comprendre) pas. Il répète: _____ (apprendre)

le français!

◄ 4.20 ►
Structure grammaticale

Les pronoms accentués · *Stressed/emphatic pronouns*

In the dialogue, Jennifer says:

> Pour moi un Perrier-citron *A lemon Perrier for me and*
> et pour lui une blonde. *a lager for him.*

Moi, toi, and **lui** are stressed pronouns. They follow a preposition.

Pour moi, une bouteille de vin rouge.	*For me, a bottle of red wine.*
Elle ne mange pas **avec toi.**	*She does not eat with you.*
Elle mange **avec lui.**	*She eats with him.*

Stressed pronouns are used to emphasize that the subject of the verb ("I, you, he, she, we, they") is involved in doing something, as opposed to someone else.

Stressed pronouns are also used to emphasize a subject pronoun. In this role, it is not translated in English.

Elle, elle adore faire les antiquaires.	*She loves to visit antique stores.*
Nous, nous assistons à un congrès médical.	*We attend/are attending a medical convention.*
Vous, vous apprenez le français.	*You are learning French.*
Eux, ils visitent Notre-Dame.	*They visit Notre-Dame.*
Elles, elles restent à l'hôtel.	*They stay in the hotel.*

They are also used without a verb.

Tu prends le train? **Moi** aussi.	*You take the train? So do I (Me too).*
Il adore le saucisson sec, et Pierre? **Lui** aussi.	*He loves salami, and Pierre? So does he.*

 ◄ **4.21** ►
Audio exercise

You are in a café with friends. The waiter on the recording wants to clarify your order. You will choose the same order for the people with you as you choose for yourself. Repeat the correct response.

EXAMPLE

PROMPT Vous prenez un sandwich au jambon. Et Monsieur?

RESPONSE Lui, il prend un sandwich au jambon aussi.

◄ 4.22 ►
Exercise

Complete the following sentences with the appropriate stressed pronoun: **moi, toi, lui, elle, nous, vous, eux, elles.**

1. _____, je suis de Bretagne.

2. Il déteste l'eau minérale gazeuse et elle? _____ aussi.

3. Christiane prend l'autobus et Fabienne et Bruno?

   _____ aussi.

4. _____, nous visitons Annecy.

5. Ma chérie danse avec _____!

6. _____, vous prenez un taxi.

7. _____, tu es en pleine forme.

8. _____, nous apprenons le français et _____, ils apprennent l'italien.

◄ 4.23 ►
Dialogue 3
Quelle heure est-il? · *What time is it?*

Our friends are still at the Deux Magots enjoying their drinks.

Nos amis sont toujours aux Deux Magots à apprécier leurs boissons.

JEREMY	Quelle heure est-il?
JENNIFER	Il est midi.
M. JONES	J'ai sommeil.
JEREMY	Moi aussi, c'est le décalage horaire.
JENNIFER	Tu as l'adresse de l'hôtel?
JEREMY	Oui, 31, non, pardon, 51 boulevard de Rennes. Demandons l'addition au serveur. Monsieur, c'est combien pour les boissons?
LE SERVEUR	Un instant, Messieurs-dames.

(Le temps passe.)

JENNIFER	Mais qu'est-ce qu'il fait?
M. JONES	Regardez, il est très occupé.

(Le garçon arrive.)

LE SERVEUR	Ah voilà, ça fait six euros quarante-sept.
JEREMY	Payons et prenons encore un taxi pour aller à l'hôtel.

◄ **4.24** ►
Petit lexique

l'adresse (*f.*)	*address*
arriver	*to arrive*
ça fait	*it costs; it is*
C'est combien?	*How much is it?*
le décalage horaire	*time lag, jet lag*
demander	*to ask*
un instant	*a minute*
midi	*midday, noon*
occupé(e)	*busy*
pardon	*excuse me, pardon*
passer	*to pass*
payer	*to pay*
le temps	*time*
voici/voilà	*here is/there is*

◄ **4.25** ►
Compréhension et expressions

Comptons! · *Let's count!*

Jennifer asks for the hotel address, and Jeremy tells her:

Trente et un, non, pardon, cinquante et un boulevard de Rennes.	*Thirty-one, no, sorry, fifty-one Boulevard de Rennes.*

Le garçon gives them the bill.

Six euros quarante-sept.	*Six euros forty-seven.*

In the previous chapter, you learned the numbers from 1 to 12. Let's continue.

13 treize
14 quatorze
15 quinze
16 seize
17 dix-sept ("x" pronounced /s/)
18 dix-huit ("x" pronounced /z/)
19 dix-neuf ("x" pronounced /z/)
20 vingt ("t" not pronounced)
21 vingt et un ("t" of **vingt** pronounced)

22 vingt-deux ("t" pronounced)
23 vingt-trois ("t" pronounced)
24 vingt-quatre ("t" pronounced)
…
30 trente
31 trente et un
32 trente-deux
…
40 quarante
41 quarante et un
42 quarante-deux
…
50 cinquante
51 cinquante et un
52 cinquante-deux
…
60 soixante ("x" pronounced /s/)

 ◄ **4.26** ►
Audio exercise

Look carefully at each row of numbers. As each number is spoken, circle it and repeat it immediately after the speaker.

1.	1	12	27	48	53	2
2.	60	29	12	33	54	11
3.	3	22	50	13	20	4
4.	44	3	34	5	51	37
5.	19	9	36	17	43	8
6.	17	6	2	77	30	56

◄ **4.27** ►
Audio exercise

In chapter 3, you learned that **avoir** is used for telling someone's age. On the recording, you will be asked someone's age in French, then prompted with the answer in English. Reply in French, then repeat the correct answer.

EXAMPLE

PROMPT Tu as quel âge? (I am fifteen.)

RESPONSE J'ai quinze ans.

◄ **4.28** ►
Compréhension et expressions

Quelle heure est-il? · *What time is it?*

In the previous chapter, you learned how to tell time on the hour. When Jeremy asks **Quelle heure est-il?**, Jennifer replies, **Il est midi**.

To express 12 o'clock noon, you say **midi**, and for 12 o'clock midnight you say **minuit**.

The acronyms A.M. and P.M. are not used in French. Instead, use the following phrases.

... du matin	*in the morning*
... de l'après-midi	*in the afternoon*
... du soir	*in the evening*

 Il est sept heures du matin à Montréal.

 Il est une heure de l'après-midi à Nice.

 Il est huit heures du soir à Tokyo.

To express the quarter hours you say:

... et quart	*quarter past*
... quinze	*fifteen*
... moins le quart	*quarter to*
... quarante-cinq	*forty-five*

6:15	Il est six heures **et quart**.
	Il est six heures **quinze**.
5:45	Il est six heures **moins le quart**.
	Il est cinq heures **quarante-cinq**.
12:15 P.M.	Il est midi **et quart**.
12:15 A.M.	Il est minuit **et quart**.

To say that it is half past the hour, add **et demi(e)** or **trente**.

7:30	Il est sept heures **et demie** à Berlin.
9:30	Il est neuf heures **trente** à Moscou.

If the minutes fall between the hour and the half hour, say the number of minutes after the hour.

9:10	Il est neuf heures dix.
2:25	Il est deux heures vingt-cinq.

If the minutes fall after the half hour, say either **moins** and the number of minutes to be subtracted from the next hour, or say the number of minutes after the hour.

8:35	Il est neuf heures **moins vingt-cinq**.
	Il est huit heures **trente-cinq**.
1:40	Il est deux heures **moins vingt**.
	Il est une heure **quarante**.

Les 24 heures · *The 24-hour system (military time)*

The twenty-four–hour system is used in all official announcements in France, such as at airports, banks, and theaters. In this system, the fractions of the hour are always expressed in terms of minutes after the hour.

sept heures dix du soir	=	dix-neuf heures dix
onze heures et demie du soir	=	vingt-trois heures trente

◄ **4.29** ►
Audio exercise

Look at the clocks below, and answer the questions on the recording about the time in each city. Then, repeat the correct answer after the speaker.

EXAMPLE

PROMPT   Quelle heure est-il à New York?
RESPONSE   À New York, il est trois heures dix.

1. Londres   2. Moscou   3. La Nouvelle Orléans

4. San Francisco   5. Tokio   6. Genève

◄ **4.30** ►
Exercise

Look again at the clocks above, and write the time in words using the 24-hour system.

EXAMPLE   Quelle heure est-il à La Nouvelle-Orléans?

     Il est treize heures trente.

1. Quelle heure est-il à Londres?

_____

2. Quelle heure est-il à San Francisco?

_____

3. Quelle heure est-il à New York?

_____

4. Quelle heure est-il à Genève?

_____

5. Quelle heure est-il à Moscou?

_____

6. Quelle heure est-il à Tokio?

_____

◄ 4.31 ►
Structure grammaticale

Verbe irrégulier *faire* · *Irregular verb* **faire** *("to do"; "to make")*

C'est combien?, Ça fait combien?	*How much is it?*
C'est..., Ça fait...	*It costs . . .*

Jennifer asks the waiter, **C'est combien pour les boissons?** ("How much are the drinks?"), and he answers, **Ça fait six euros quarante-sept** ("It's 6 euros 47").

The basic meaning of **faire** is "to do" or "to make." However, like the irregular verbs **être** and **avoir**, **faire** is used in many expressions where a different verb is used in English. In Chapter 2 you saw expressions with **faire** that are used to talk about the weather. Now look at these further examples of usage.

Faites comme chez vous. Fais comme chez toi. }	*Make yourself at home.*
Ne vous en faites pas! Ne t'en fais pas! }	*Don't worry!*
Ça ne fait rien.	*It doesn't matter.*
Qu'est-ce que vous faites?	*What are you doing?*
Je fais une réservation.	*I am making a reservation.*
Tu fais la sieste.	*You take a nap.*
Il fait un bisou.	*He gives a kiss.*
Elle fait un gâteau.	*She is baking a cake.*
Nous faisons un tour.	*We are going for a ride.*
Vous faites une promenade.	*You take a walk.*
Faites le plein!	*Fill up the tank!*
Ils font du shopping.	*They go shopping.*

Faire du sport · *To play (to do, to practice) a sport*

Quels sports tu fais?	*Which sports do you do/practice?*
J'aime beaucoup le tennis,	*I like tennis, fencing, and sailing*
l'escrime et la voile.	*a lot. In the morning I play*
Le matin, je fais **du**	*tennis; at night I fence at the*
tennis, le soir je fais **de**	*club. In the summer I go*
l'escrime au club. L'été,	*sailing.*
je fais **de la** voile.	

NOTE: **Du** is used if the noun is masculine, **de l'** if it starts with a vowel, and **de la** if it is feminine. The silent **h** in **hockey** is treated like a consonant: **il fait du hockey**.

◄ 4.32 ►
Audio exercise

On the recording, you will be asked in French whether you or someone else likes a particular sport. Reply by saying that you or that person does play the sport.

EXAMPLE

PROMPT   Vous aimez le karaté?

RESPONSE   Oui, je fais du karaté.

◄ 4.33 ►
Exercise

Catherine is on vacation in Nice, and she is sending an e-mail to her friend in Boston. Complete the message with the correct form of **faire** and the correct article when necessary.

Salut Anne,

Quel temps _____-il à Boston? Le matin,

à Nice, il _____ soleil. Je _____

natation et Antoine _____ tennis. L'après-midi,

il pleut souvent mais ça ne _____ rien; nous

_____ sieste. Le soir, j'aime _____

shopping. Quelquefois on _____ tour.

Ne t'en _____ pas pour moi. Je suis en pleine

forme. _____ bisou aux amis. À bientôt!

Catherine

◄ 4.34 ►
Common pitfalls

Listen to the class interaction between the student and the teacher on the recording. They are role-playing a scene in a restaurant, with the teacher playing the part of the waiter.

This interaction shows us how easy it is to get into difficulties when traveling abroad, simply by mispronouncing one syllable or even a single letter. Here the student-customer is asking for dessert, but pronounces /day-zair/, **le désert**, which in French applies to a wide, open, dry, barren land, so the teacher-waiter does not understand and is puzzled. The proper pronunciation for **le dessert** ("dessert" in English) is /day-sair/. Many words, especially cognates, can lead to such difficulties. To avoid embarrassment, it is important to pay close attention when you hear the pronunciation of words and when you imitate.

◄ 4.35 ►
Let's take a plunge!

Using what you have learned in this chapter, answer the speaker on the recording in a spontaneous conversation.

◄ 4.36 ►
Vive la différence!

Paris

> "If you are lucky enough to have lived in Paris as a young man, then wherever you go for the rest of your life, it stays with you, for Paris is a moveable feast."
> —Ernest Hemingway

Paris is still the heart of French life despite recent French governments' efforts to decentralize the capital. Beyond the City of Lights are the provinces. The distinction between the two has created a sort of love-hate relationship between **les Parisiens** and **les provinciaux**, a little like New Yorkers who see only Manhattan: everything west of the Hudson River is the rest of the world!

Paris used to be called **Lutèce** before the Romans invaded it around 50 B.C. The name Paris comes from the name of the tribe that lived in the area at the time, the "Parisis."

Cafés

Cafés first came into existence in the second half of the seventeenth century because of the new fad of Arabian coffee. They multiplied rapidly, and during the eighteenth century they became the place where people would meet to play chess and discuss politics and philosophy. The oldest café in Paris is the Procope, which was established in 1686 and still operates today. It was already one hundred years old when Benjamin Franklin visited it.

French cafés serve all kinds of soft drinks, hot drinks, wines, beers, and spirits, and often offer snacks and sometimes full meals. They are an important part of French life, where friends meet to converse and to argue and where people sit to study or just to watch life pass by on the sidewalks.

Bars serve coffee, alcoholic drinks, and sometimes light meals.

Bistro(t)s, the origin of which is anything but French, were introduced into France by Napoleon's troops after their campaign in Russia. The word comes from the Russian "bistra," which means "hurry." Today, a **bistro(t)** is a typical French establishment where you can find not only drinks but homemade **plats du jour**.

Le pourboire *(literally, "to get a drink")* · *Tipping*

Most French restaurants and hotels add a 10 to 15 percent service charge to the check, as well as government tax. This is referred to as **service compris** or **toutes taxes comprises**. You may wish to add a little extra tip if the service has been particularly good.

◄ 4.37 ►
How to make it sound French

FRENCH LETTER COMBINATION	EXAMPLE WORDS	PRONUNCIATION
-ch-	château, enchanté	like *sh* in sheep
-tion	addition	"t" is pronounced /s/

Some French letters aren't pronounced at all.

h-	(h)ôtel, (h)eure, (h)abiter	
-c at the end of a word	vin blan(c), bureau de taba(c)	

À l'hôtel

At the hotel

OBJECTIVE

In this chapter, you check in at the hotel reception desk. There, you are faced with unexpected problems. Don't forget to make that phone call to Cannes. Keep working on the euro system; prices always seem to be higher than you think. . . .

◄ 5.1 ►
DIALOGUE 1
À la réception · *At the reception desk*

Our three friends have left the Deux Magots and have arrived at
the hotel. They are now checking in at the reception desk.

Nos trois amis ont quitté Les Deux Magots et sont arrivés à l'hôtel.
Ils sont à la réception.

RÉCEPTIONNISTE	Bonjour Messieurs-dames.
LES TROIS	Bonjour Mademoiselle.
RÉCEPTIONNISTE	Est-ce que je peux vous aider?
JENNIFER	Nous avons une réservation pour trois chambres.
RÉCEPTIONNISTE	À quel nom?
JENNIFER	M. Jones.
RÉCEPTIONNISTE	Je suis désolée, je n'ai pas trois chambres, mais une chambre double et une chambre simple côté cour.
M. JONES	Mais c'est impossible!
RÉCEPTIONNISTE	Avez-vous la confirmation de la réservation?
M. JONES	Oui, la voici: trois chambres.

◄ 5.2 ►
Petit lexique

aider	*to help*
avoir besoin de/d'	*to need*
la chambre	*room; hotel room*
la chambre climatisée	*air-conditioned room*
la chambre double	*double room*
la chambre simple	*single room*
la confirmation	*confirmation*
le côté	*side*
le côté cour	*overlooking the courtyard*
le côté rue	*overlooking the street*
désolé(e)	*sorry*
donner sur	*to open onto, to face (said of a building or a window)*
impossible	*impossible*
le nom	*name*
je peux	*I can*
pouvoir	*to be able to, can*
la réception	*reception desk*

Extension de vocabulaire

l'ampoule (*f.*)	*lightbulb*
la chaise	*chair*
la clé	*key*
le fauteuil	*armchair*
la fenêtre	*window*
l'interrupteur (*m.*)	*light switch*
la porte	*door*
la couverture	*blanket*
le drap	*bedsheet*
le lit	*bed*
l'oreiller (*m.*)	*pillow*
le traversin	*bolster (pillow)*
la baignoire	*bathtub*
la douche	*shower*
l'eau chaude (*f.*)	*hot water*
l'eau froide (*f.*)	*cold water*
prendre une douche	*to take a shower*
la salle de bains	*bathroom*
le gant de toilette	*facecloth, washcloth*
la serviette de bain	*bath towel*
la serviette de toilette	*hand towel*
la brosse à dents	*toothbrush*
le dentifrice	*toothpaste*
les effets de toilette (*m.pl.*)	*toiletries*
le papier hygiénique	*toilet paper*
le rasoir	*razor*
la savonnette	*bath soap*
le séchoir à cheveux	*hair dryer*

◄ 5.3 ►

Compréhension et expressions

Est-ce que je peux vous aider? · *May I help you?*

We already know that when meeting a person we say **bonjour** in French. But if you enter a store or a restaurant, you will also hear:

Bonjour (Monsieur/Madame/   *Good day (sir, madam, miss),*
     Mademoiselle) est-ce que   *may I/can I help you?*
     je peux vous aider?

être désolé · *to be sorry*

Je suis désolé(e) is used to apologize informally for a situation one cannot control. The French also say **Pardon, Pardonnez-moi,** and **Excusez-moi.**

Oui, la voici! · *Yes, here it is!*

Vous avez la clé?   *Do you have the key?*
Oui, la voici.   *Yes, here it is.*

◄ 5.4 ►
Structure grammaticale

Formation de questions · *Formulating questions*

Est-ce que...?

You have learned how to ask a question by raising the tone of your voice. Now, notice that the receptionist is saying, **Est-ce que je peux vous aider?** ("Can/May I help you?").

To ask a question, you can add **Est-ce que?** in front of a statement.

Jennifer a une réservation.
Est-ce que Jennifer a une réservation?

Vous avez trois chambres.
Est-ce que vous avez trois chambres?

Inversion

As we continue the dialogue, the receptionist asks, **Avez-vous la confirmation de la réservation?**

Another way of asking a question is to invert the order of the verb and the subject pronoun. With the inversion, you must place a hyphen between the verb and the subject pronoun.

Vous avez une réservation.   **Avez-vous** une réservation?

Note that the inversion is only possible with a subject pronoun. When the subject is a noun, insert the appropriate pronoun in the inversion following the noun.

Jennifer a une réservation.
Jennifer a-t-elle une réservation?

Note that a -t- is added in the inversion if the verb ends in a vowel; this prevents the jarring sound of two vowels together.

◄ 5.5 ►
Audio exercise

Let's play Jeopardy! Listen to each of the following prompts, then ask the appropriate question using **Est-ce que?** Repeat the correct question after the speaker.

EXAMPLE

PROMPT   J'ai une réservation.

RESPONSE   Est-ce que vous avez une réservation?

◄ 5.6 ►
Exercise

Transform the following statements into questions using inversion.

EXAMPLE   Vous avez une réservation.

   Avez-vous une réservation?

1. Vous avez une chambre climatisée.

   _____

2. Vous avez une chambre double.

   _____

3. Vous avez un sauna.

   _____

4. Jennifer a une réservation.

   _____

5. Nous jouons au basket.

   _____

6. Jennifer et M. Jones désirent un Perrier-citron.

   _____

7. Nous aimons la tour Eiffel

_____

8. Le président français habit

_____

9. Nous avons des amis.

_____

10. Nous avons une salle de b

_____

 ◄ 5.7 ►
DIALOGUE 2
Un problème de réservati

Our friends are still at the rec
misunderstanding regarding th

Nos amis sont toujours à la réce
soudre un petit malentendu con

M. JONES	Oui, trois chambr
RÉCEPTIONNISTE	Ah! La réservatio
	l'ordinateur!
JEREMY	Mais comment ce
	chambres, parc
RÉCEPTIONNISTE	Encore une fois,
	chambres pour
	pour ce soir et
	trois chambres
M. JONES	Et pourquoi pas
RÉCEPTIONNISTE	Mais Monsieur, c
	beaucoup de t
M. JONES	Ah c'est vrai, c'e

◄ 5.8 ►
Petit lexique

beaucoup (de)
ce/cette
Comment cela?
complet/complète

_____

e à l'Élysée.

_____

_____

ins.

_____

on · *A reservation problem*

ption desk trying to work out a
eir reservation.

ption de l'hôtel. Ils essaient de ré-
ernant leur réservation.

s pour le 12, 13 et 14 juillet!
: G XJ-75 81-98 n'est pas dans

ia! Nous, nous devons avoir trois
e que nous avons une réservation.
onsieur, j'ai seulement deux
la nuit du 14, mais si vous voulez,
demain mardi vous pouvez avoir

our le quatorze aussi?
est le 14 Juillet, nous avons
uristes et l'hôtel est complet.
t la fête nationale française.

much, many, a lot
this; that
How come? What?
full

NOTE: In French (unlike English), the months of the year and the days of the week are not capitalized except in the case of holidays and religious feasts.

◄ **5.9** ►
Compréhension et expressions

Comptons encore! · *Let's count again!*

We have learned to count up to sixty. Let's continue.

60 soixante ("x" pronounced /s/)
61 soixante et un
62 soixante deux

For the seventies, you need to be good at mental arithmetic! You will add 10–19 to sixty.

70 soixante-dix
71 soixante et onze
72 soixante-douze
73 soixante-treize
74 soixante-quatorze
75 soixante-quinze
76 soixante-seize
77 soixante-dix-sept
78 soixante-dix-huit
79 soixante-dix-neuf

For the eighties, add **un, deux, trois**, etc. to 80 (use **quatre-vingt—quatre-vingts** minus the **-s**).

80 quatre-vingts (that is, 4 × 20)
81 quatre-vingt-un (no **et** before **un**)
82 quatre-vingt-deux

For the nineties add **dix, onze, douze**, as we did for the seventies.

90 quatre-vingt-dix (that is, 4 × 20 + 10)
91 quatre-vingt-onze
92 quatre-vingt-douze

The hundreds and thousands are straightforward.

100	cent
101	cent un
102	cent deux
130	cent trente
160	cent soixante
180	cent quatre-vingts
200	deux cents
300	trois cents
900	neuf cents
998	neuf cent quatre-vingt-dix-huit
1000	mille
1538	mille cinq cent trente-huit

◄ **5.10** ►
Audio exercise

Listen to the recording. Repeat the numbers given in pairs, and write them down in digits.

1. _____

2. _____

3. _____

4. _____

5. _____

6. _____

7. _____

8. _____

◄ 5.11 ►
Exercise

Look at the culture section on **les jours fériés** at the end of this chapter (page 96), and answer the question **Quelle est la date de** _____? ("What is the date of _____?").

EXAMPLE   Quelle est la date de la fête nationale française?

C'est le 14 Juillet.

1. Quelle est la date de la fête nationale belge?

   _____

2. Quelle est la date de l'Assomption?

   _____

3. Quelle est la date de la Victoire?

   _____

4. Quelle est la date de Noël?

   _____

5. Quelle est la date de la fête du Travail?

   _____

6. Quelle est la date de la fête nationale suisse?

   _____

7. Quelle est la date de la fête nationale américaine?

   _____

8. Quelle est la date de la Toussaint?

   _____

◄ 5.12 ►
Compréhension et expressions

encore une fois · *one more time, once again*

Encore une fois, tu as raison!   *Once again, you are right!*

C'est vrai. · *It's true., You're right.*

C'est vrai, Paris est une très   *It's true; Paris is a beautiful*
   belle ville!   *city!*

C'est complet. · *It's full.*

> Nous ne pouvons pas aller au théâtre ce soir, c'est complet!

> *We cannot go to the theater tonight; it's sold out (full)!*

You will hear or see this expression in cinemas, theaters, concert halls, hotels, restaurants, and when making travel reservations. It means "It's full./There is no more room./No vacancies./Sold out."

> L'avion est complet.
> Le concert de Chopin est complet.

> *The plane is full.*
> *The Chopin concert is sold out.*

Comment cela!? · *How come!?*

The common expression **Comment cela?** or **Comment?** expresses surprise on the part of the speaker and is the equivalent of "What?" or "I/We don't get it!" in English. Study the following examples.

> Comment cela, le musée est fermé!
> Mais oui, c'est juillet.

> *I don't get it! The museum is closed!*
> *Well, sure. It's July.*

> Jennifer est américaine.
> Comment? Elle n'est pas française?

> *Jennifer is American.*
> *What? She's not French?*

◄ 5.13 ►
Structure grammaticale

Verbes irréguliers · *Irregular verbs*

> vouloir ("to want/wish/can")
> pouvoir ("to be able to/can/may")
> devoir ("to have to/must")

These three important irregular verbs express

- desire/wish (**vouloir**)

> Je **veux** aller au cinéma.
> Nous **voulons** un coca-cola.

> *I want to go to the movies.*
> *We want a Coca-Cola.*

- possibility/ability (**pouvoir**)

  Il **peut** parler français. *He can speak French.*
  Vous **pouvez** acheter une *You can buy a phone card at*
   télécarte au bureau de tabac. *the tobacco shop.*

- obligation (**devoir**)

  Tu **dois** comprendre les *You have to understand*
   mathématiques.   *math.*
  Combien est-ce que je vous *How much do I owe you for*
   dois pour l'appel?   *the call?*

NOTE: In French, as in English, when one verb follows another, it takes the infinitive form. **Vouloir** and **devoir** can also be followed by a noun. In the case of **devoir**, the meaning becomes "to owe."

VOULOIR ("to want"; "to wish")

je **veux**	Je **veux** partir. *I want to leave.*
tu **veux**	Tu **veux** manger une orange. *You want to eat an orange.*
il/elle/on **veut**	Elle **veut** une orange. *She wants an orange.*
nous **voulons**	Nous **voulons** un taxi. *We want a taxi.*
vous **voulez**	**Voulez**-vous un thé? *Do you want a cup of tea?*
ils/elles **veulent**	Ils ne **veulent** pas aller à Rome. *They do not want to go to Rome.*

POUVOIR ("to be able to"; "can")

je **peux**	Je **peux** parler français. *I can speak French.*
tu **peux**	Tu **peux** compter jusqu'à trente. *You can count up to thirty.*
il/elle/on **peut**	Il **peut** étudier le français à Paris. *He can study French in Paris.*

nous **pouvons**	Nous **pouvons** utiliser l'ordinateur. *We can use the computer.*
vous **pouvez**	Vous **pouvez** voir la Joconde au Louvre. *You can see the Mona Lisa in the Louvre.*
ils/elles **peuvent**	Elles **peuvent** skier. *They can ski.*

DEVOIR ("to have to"; "must")

je **dois**	Je **dois** aller chez le dentiste. *I must go to the dentist.*
tu **dois**	**Dois**-tu aller à Montréal? *Must you go to Montreal?*
il/elle/on **doit**	On ne **doit** pas fumer au cinéma. *One must not smoke in the movie theater.*
nous **devons**	Nous **devons** cent euros à la banque. *We owe one hundred euros to the bank.*
vous **devez**	Vous **devez** partir en Algérie. *You have to leave for Algeria.*
ils/elles **doivent**	Ils **doivent** aller au restaurant. *They must go to the restaurant.*

Remember, **devoir** means "to owe" when followed by a noun.

 ◄ **5.14** ►
Audio exercise

Listen to the questions, and answer in the affirmative with the appropriate form of **vouloir**, **pouvoir**, or **devoir**. Then, repeat the correct answer after the speaker.

EXAMPLE

PROMPT   Voulez-vous un thé?
RESPONSE   Je veux un thé.

◄ 5.15 ►
Audio exercise

Listen again to the speaker (who uses **vouloir**) and tell him that you want to accept his offer, but you cannot (using **pouvoir**). Then, repeat the correct response after the speaker.

EXAMPLE

PROMPT   Voulez-vous aller au cinéma?
RESPONSE Je veux mais je ne peux pas.

◄ 5.16 ►
Audio exercise

Answer the questions as prompted, using the three verbs you have learned: **vouloir**, **pouvoir**, and **devoir**. Then, repeat the correct answer after the speaker.

EXAMPLE

PROMPT   Devez-vous aller chez le dentiste?
            (I must, but I don't want to.)
RESPONSE Je dois, mais je ne veux pas.

◄ 5.17 ►
Exercise

Complete the following sentences with the correct form of the verb in parentheses.

1. Jennifer _____ visiter la Dordogne.
   (vouloir)

2. Vous _____ utiliser une télécarte.
   (pouvoir) (une télécarte, *phone card*)

3. Jeremy _____ une chambre simple.
   (vouloir)

4. Les amis _____ avoir une réservation.
   (devoir)

5. Est-ce que je _____ vous aider? (pouvoir)

6. Ils _____ partir en Tunisie. (devoir)

7. Je _____ deux euros à mon ami. (devoir)

8. On ne _____ pas parler dans le théâtre. (devoir)

9. Elles _____ utiliser l'Internet. (pouvoir) (utiliser, *to use*)

10. Nous _____ aller au festival de Cannes. (vouloir)

◄ 5.18 ►
Exercise

Complete the following sentences, choosing the correct form of one of the three verbs: **vouloir**, **devoir**, and **pouvoir**. Be sure your choice of verb is logical.

1. Jennifer et Jeremy _____ prendre un taxi pour aller à l'arc de Triomphe.

2. M. Jones _____ cinq euros à Jennifer.

3. Jennifer _____ boire un Orangina.

4. Il ne _____ pas parler italien, mais il

   _____ parler français.

5. _____-vous un café ou un thé?

6. Les enfants _____ obéir aux parents. (obéir, *to obey*)

7. Dans l'avion, on ne _____ pas utiliser de mobile. (le mobile, *cell phone*)

8. Jennifer veut déjeuner à la Tour d'Argent, mais Jeremy et

   M. Jones ne _____ pas.

9. On _____ avoir un passeport pour voyager.

10. Elles _____ un billet de loterie. (un billet de loterie, *a lottery ticket*)

◄ 5.19 ►

DIALOGUE 3
Jennifer téléphone à Cannes · *Jennifer phones Cannes*

Listen to the conversation between Jennifer and the hotel receptionist.

Écoutez la conversation entre Jennifer et la réceptionniste.

JENNIFER	Mademoiselle, est-ce que je peux téléphoner à Cannes?
RÉCEPTIONNISTE	Sans problème. Avez-vous le numéro?
JENNIFER	Oui, c'est le 78.29.37.16.
RÉCEPTIONNISTE	Avez-vous l'indicatif pour Cannes?
JENNIFER	Non!
RÉCEPTIONNISTE	Attention, c'est le « 04 »...
JENNIFER	Mademoiselle, combien est-ce que je vous dois pour l'appel?
RÉCEPTIONNISTE	2,92 euros, Mademoiselle.
JENNIFER	C'est assez cher. Voici cinq euros!
RÉCEPTIONNISTE	Alors, 2,92 et deux, ça fait quatre euros quatre-vingt-douze et huit centimes, ça fait cinq euros. Vous pouvez utiliser une télécarte, c'est plus économique.
JENNIFER	Avez-vous des télécartes à vendre?
RÉCEPTIONNISTE	Non, Mademoiselle, je regrette, mais pour acheter des télécartes vous devez aller au bureau de tabac ou au bar.

Listen again to the dialogue, and repeat after the speaker. Then listen a third time, pausing the recording, so that you can first play the role of the receptionist and then the part of Jennifer.

◄ 5.20 ►
Petit lexique

l'appel (*m.*)	*phone call*
le bar	*bar*
bon marché	*cheap, inexpensive*
le bureau de tabac	*tobacco shop*
cher/chère	*expensive; dear*
la communication	*phone call*

économique	*economical*
l'indicatif (*m.*)	*area code*
le numéro	*number*
plus	*more*
le problème	*problem*
regretter	*to regret*
sans	*without*
la télécarte	*phone card*
téléphoner	*to telephone*
vendre	*to sell*

 ◄ 5.21 ►
Common pitfalls

Listen to the class interaction on the recording as a student tries to tell the teacher about a doctor's appointment.

As explained earlier in this chapter, when **devoir** is followed by a preposition (rather than a verb of action), it means "to owe somebody something," and it no longer expresses obligation or demand. So when the student states **Je dois au docteur**, the teacher assumes that the student is trying to tell her how much he owes the doctor. Finally, the teacher understands the student's mistake and explains how to say that one has to go to the doctor at two o'clock: **Ah, vous devez aller chez le docteur à deux heures. Je dois aller.**

 ◄ 5.22 ►
Let's take a plunge!

Study Dialogue 3 again carefully, then answer the questions about Jennifer on the recording.

◄ 5.23 ►
Vive la différence!

Les jours fériés · *French holidays*

The French enjoy a number of official holidays during the course of the year. They plan ahead of time to **faire le pont** (literally, "to make the bridge"), that is, to make the best of these short breaks by taking an extended weekend. For example, if the holiday falls on a Tuesday, the French will take Monday off as well, thus bridging from Sunday to Tuesday.

Le jour de l'An	*New Year's Day (January 1)*
Le lundi de Pâques	*Easter Monday*
Le 1er (premier) mai (le jour du Travail)	*Labor Day (May 1)*
Le 8 (huit) mai (le jour de la Victoire)	*Victory Day (May 8)*
L'Ascension	*Ascension Day (in May)*
Le lundi de la Pentecôte	*Whitmonday (in May or June)*
La Fête Nationale	*Bastille Day (July 14)*
L'Assomption	*Assumption Day (August 15)*
La Toussaint	*All Saints' Day (November 1)*
Le 11 (onze) novembre	*Armistice Day (November 11)*
Noël	*Christmas Day (December 25)*

National holidays

in France	July 14
in Belgium	July 21
in Switzerland	August 1
in Quebec	June 24

July 14, 1789: This is probably the most important date in the history of France. It was the day of the storming of the Bastille, the royal prison, a symbolic event that marked the beginning of the French Revolution, soon to be followed by the rise of the Republic.

July 21, 1831: For centuries, Belgium fought for its independence from France and then from the Netherlands. Yet it was declared a free and separate state only on October 4, 1830. The first king of Belgium, Leopold I, was crowned on July 21, 1831.

August 1: Independence for Switzerland came when the Holy Roman Emperor, Rudolf of Habsburg, died in 1291. On August 1 of that year, the elders of the three small communities of Schwyz, Uri, and Unterwalden met and declared their right to self-government. This pact was the foundation of the Swiss Confederation.

June 24, 1834: French roots in North America go back to 1534, when Jacques Cartier claimed the province of Quebec for France. Samuel de Champlain established the first trading post that eventually would become the city of Quebec.

Today the **Québécois** are proud of their French heritage and express their sentiment in the official motto of the province: **Je**

me souviens. The fleur-de-lis, shown on the flag and on automobile registration plates, is the symbol of the province.

◄ **5.24** ►
How to make it sound French

Élision

Certain one-syllable words ending in a vowel drop the vowel when they precede words beginning with a vowel or silent **h**; an apostrophe replaces the dropped vowel. This phenomenon, called **élision**, is important in French pronunciation. It occurs

- with a number of words ending in -e (**ce, de, je, le, me, ne, que, te**)

  Je **n'**aime pas le thé.   *I don't like tea.*

  Note the **élision** of the **e** (the vowel -**e** is dropped) of **ne** when it precedes the first letter **a**- of the verb **aimer**.

- with **si** before **il/ils**

  S'il vous plaît.   *Please. (If it pleases you.)*

Nasal sounds

Nasal sounds occur when a vowel is followed by **n** or **m**. The sounds are made slightly through the nose as if you had a cold.

FRENCH SOUND AND EXAMPLE WORDS	NEAREST ENGLISH SOUND
-**am**, chambre; -**an**, restaurant -**em**, ensemble; -**en**, encore -**om**, complet; -**on**, pardon	-*ong* as in "son(g)" without the "g"
-**im**, impossible; -**in**, vin -**ain**, demain, -**ein**, hein -**ien**, bien, italien	-*ang* as in "ban(g)" without the "g"
-**um**, parfum; -**un**, un café	-*an* as in "an (apple)"

If a word ends in a nasal sound with **n**, a **liaison** usually occurs when the next word starts with a vowel or silent **h**.

un‿homme   pronounced un /n/homme
un‿ami   pronounced un /n/ami

◄ 6 ►

Au Procope
At the Procope

OBJECTIVE

You have finally settled down in your hotel. Today you are going to enjoy lunch in a famous Parisian restaurant, although you may encounter difficulties giving your order. What about tomorrow? Expand your knowledge of French by learning the immediate future tense, a new group of regular verbs, and some irregular ones.

◄ 6.1 ►
DIALOGUE 1
Une table près de la fenêtre · *A table near the window*

Our three friends are now having lunch at a landmark restaurant, the Procope. Listen to their conversation with the maître d' as they request a table for three.

Nos trois amis déjeunent dans un restaurant célèbre, le Procope. Écoutons leur conversation avec le maître d'hôtel; ils demandent une table pour trois personnes.

MAITRE D'HOTEL	Messieurs-dames!
M. JONES	Une table pour trois personnes, s'il vous plaît!
MAITRE D'HOTEL	Trois couverts, par ici, s'il vous plaît.
JENNIFER	Pouvons-nous avoir une table près de la fenêtre?
MAITRE D'HOTEL	Tout à fait, Mademoiselle.

Listen one more time to the conversation between the maître d' and our friends.

Now you will play the part of the maître d'.

◄ 6.2 ►
Petit lexique

le couvert	*place setting*
par ici	*this way, over here*
près de	*near*
tout à fait	*absolutely, completely*

◄ 6.3 ►
Compréhension et expressions

Demander une table · *Asking for a table*

When you go into a French restaurant, you may ask for **une table pour trois (personnes)** or simply for **trois couverts** ("three place settings").

You may also hear the server say **Par ici**, which means "This way/Over here," or **Suivez-moi**, "Follow me."

◄ 6.4 ►
Audio exercise

You are in a French restaurant and will be prompted on the recording to ask for a table. Substitute the word **couvert**, and follow the model.

EXAMPLE

PROMPT   Une table pour deux.
RESPONSE   Deux couverts, s'il vous plaît.

◄ 6.5 ►
Structure grammaticale

Les prépositions · *Prepositions*

A preposition is a word that connects a noun or pronoun with a verb, adjective, or another noun or pronoun. Here are some common prepositions and examples of their use.

près de   *near*
loin de   *far from*

Pouvons-nous avoir une table près de la fenêtre?	*Can we have a table near the window?*
Une table loin de la fenêtre.	*A table far from the window.*
Versailles est près de Paris.	*Versailles is near Paris.*
New York est loin de Paris.	*New York is far from Paris.*

devant   *in front of*
derrière   *behind*
en face de   *in front of, opposite*

Une table devant la fenêtre.	*A table in front of the window.*
Le garçon derrière la table.	*The waiter behind the table.*
Le prof est devant les étudiants.	*The teacher is in front of the students.*
Le prof est derrière le bureau.	*The teacher is behind the desk.*
La statue de la Liberté est en face de Manhattan.	*The Statue of Liberty is opposite Manhattan.*

| sur | *on* |
| sous | *under* |

| Le couvert est sur la table. | *The place setting is on the table.* |
| Il n'est pas sous la table. | *It isn't under the table.* |

au milieu de/de la/ du/de l'/des	*in the middle of*
entre	*between/in between*
à côté de	*next to*

L'île de Guam est au milieu de l'océan Pacifique.	*Guam is in the middle of the Pacific Ocean.*
New York est entre Boston et Washington, D.C.	*New York is between Boston and Washington, D.C.*
Le Canada est à côté des États-Unis.	*Canada is next to (borders) the United States.*

◄ **6.6** ►
Audio exercise

Look at the picture below, and answer the questions on the recording. Pay particular attention to the prepositions. Then, repeat the correct answer after the speaker.

EXAMPLE

PROMPT   Où sont les amis?
RESPONSE Ils sont au restaurant.

◄ 6.7 ►
Exercise

Complete the following sentences with the appropriate preposition, choosing from the following.

à	près de	au milieu de	sous
au	loin de	en face de	devant
à la	à côté de	sur	derrière
de			

1. Les trois amis sont _____ Paris.

2. M. Jones n'est pas français, il vient _____ New York. (il vient, *he comes*)

3. La Belgique est _____ la France.

4. Dans un restaurant, les couverts sont _____ la table.

5. Quand il pleut, on marche _____ le parapluie. (le parapluie, *umbrella*)

6. Le criminel est _____ le juge. (le juge, *judge*)

7. Dans un avion, la classe économique est _____ la première classe. (la classe économique, *coach class*; la première classe, *first class*)

8. L'Eurostar passe _____ la Manche. (la Manche, *English Channel*)

9. Le mois de juin est _____ l'année.

10. Versailles est près de Paris, mais New York est

    _____ Paris.

◄ 6.8 ►
DIALOGUE 2
Qu'est-ce que vous allez prendre? · *What are you having?*

Our three friends have consulted the menu and are ready to order, but not without some difficulties.

Nos trois amis consultent le menu et sont prêts à commander, mais non sans problèmes.

JEREMY	Qu'est-ce que tu vas prendre comme hors-d'œuvre?
JENNIFER	Une assiette de crudités.
LA SERVEUSE	Et vous, Monsieur?
M. JONES	Des crevettes, un cocktail de crevettes.
JEREMY	Et moi, une soupe à l'oignon, s'il vous plaît.
LA SERVEUSE	Et comme plat principal?
M. JONES	Le canard à l'orange pour Mademoiselle, le lapin à la moutarde pour le jeune homme et pour moi le bœuf bourguignon.
LA SERVEUSE	Et comme boisson, Mademoiselle?
JENNIFER	Je ne veux pas de poisson, je veux une assiette de crudités et du canard à l'orange.
LA SERVEUSE	C'est d'accord Mademoiselle, une assiette de crudités et le canard à l'orange, mais comme *boisson*?
M. JONES	Mademoiselle ne veut pas de *poisson*!
JEREMY	Elle veut une assiette de crudités, de la salade, pas de poisson.
LA SERVEUSE	C'est entièrement d'accord, mais comme *boisson* (*slowly*), glou, glou, glou!
M. JONES, JEREMY ET JENNIFER	Ah *boisson*! Du vin français.

◄ **6.9** ►
Petit lexique

l'assiette (*f.*)	*plate, bowl*
le bœuf	*beef*
la boisson	*drink*
le canard	*duck*
le cocktail	*cocktail*
la crevette	*shrimp*
les crudités (*f.pl.*)	*raw vegetables*
d'accord	*all right, okay*
entièrement	*totally, entirely*
le hors-d'œuvre	*appetizer, hors d'oeuvre*
glou glou	*glug-glug*
le lapin	*rabbit*
la moutarde	*mustard*
l'oignon (*m.*)	*onion*

le plat principal	*main dish*
le poisson	*fish*
la salade	*salad*
la serveuse	*waitress*
la soupe	*soup*
le vin	*wine*

Extension de vocabulaire

le petit déjeuner	*breakfast*
le déjeuner	*lunch*
le dîner	*dinner*
le couteau	*knife*
la cuillère, la cuiller	*spoon*
la cuillère à café	*teaspoon*
la petite cuillère	*dessertspoon*
la cuillère à dessert	*dessertspoon*
la cuillère à soupe	*tablespoon*
la fourchette	*fork*
la soucoupe	*saucer*
le poivre	*pepper*
le sel	*salt*
la nappe	*tablecloth*
la serviette (de table)	*napkin*

◀ 6.10 ▶
Compréhension et expressions

Un repas français · *A typical French meal*

A typical French meal is composed of three courses: **le hors-d'œuvre** ("the appetizer"), **le plat principal** ("the main dish"), and **le dessert**. The main dish, **le plat principal**, is generally followed by salad and cheese, **la salade et le fromage**.

C'est d'accord · *It's fine, It's okay*

To express agreement, you say **C'est d'accord**, and if you want to express agreement more strongly, you say **C'est entièrement d'accord** ("It's quite alright").

◄ 6.11 ►
Structure grammaticale
Futur Immédiat · *Immediate future*

Just as in English, **aller** + infinitive ("to be going to" + verb) is used to form the immediate future. **Aller** is conjugated in the present tense. For example, in the dialogue Jennifer asks, **Qu'est-ce que tu vas prendre comme hors-d'œuvre?** ("What are you going to have as an hors d'oeuvre?").

ALLER ("to be going to")

PRESENT	IMMEDIATE FUTURE
je **vais**	Je **vais** manger. *I'm going to eat.*
tu **vas**	Tu **vas** voyager. *You're going to travel.*
il/elle/on **va**	Il **va** nager. *He's going to swim.*
nous **allons**	Nous **allons** visiter Paris. *We're going to visit Paris.*
vous **allez**	Vous **allez** cuisiner. *You're going to cook.*
ils/elles **vont**	Elles **vont** prendre l'autobus. *They're going to take the bus.*

NOTE: To form the negative of the immediate future, you place **ne** before and **pas** after the conjugated form of **aller**.

Je vais visiter la tour Eiffel; je **ne** vais **pas** visiter le Louvre.	*I am going to visit the Eiffel Tower; I am not going to visit the Louvre.*
Nous **n'**allons **pas** aller au cirque; nous allons aller au théâtre.	*We are not going to go to the circus; we are going to go to the theater.*

◄ 6.12 ►
Audio exercise

Answer the questions on the recording in the affirmative, using the immediate future.

EXAMPLE

PROMPT   Est-ce que tu vas visiter le Louvre?
RESPONSE   Oui, je vais visiter le Louvre.

◄ 6.13 ►
Structure grammaticale

Les partitifs · *Partitives*

Jennifer asks for *du* canard à l'orange and Jeremy for *de la* salade, while Mr. Jones orders *des* crevettes. Note the rules for the use of these articles.

du	*if the noun is masculine singular*
de la	*if the noun is feminine singular*
de l'	*if the noun starts with a vowel or silent* **h**
des	*if the noun is plural (masculine or feminine)*

These are partitive articles. The partitive article in French is used to express an indefinite amount of something: "some" or "any." In English, it is common to say "coffee, please" when you really mean "some coffee." Unlike in English, partitive articles are never omitted in French.

Je voudrais **du** vin français, **de la** moutarde de Dijon et **des** escargots de Bourgogne.

I would like (some) French wine, (some) Dijon mustard, and (some) snails from Burgundy.

Négation du partitif et de l'indéfini · *Negative partitive and indefinite articles*

Did you notice that Jennifer says, **Je ne veux** *pas de* poisson? This is because in the negative, **du, de la, de l'**, and **des** become **de** or **d'**. The same rule applies to the indefinite article: **un, une, des** (see page 65, Chapter 4).

Vous prenez **du** vin?
Non, je ne prends **pas de** vin.

Voulez-vous **de la** salade?
Non, je ne veux **pas de** salade.

Voulez-vous **un** café?
Non, je ne veux **pas de** café.

Désirez-vous **une** glace?
Non, je ne veux **pas de** glace.

Mangez-vous **des** chocolats après le dîner?
Non, je ne mange **pas de** chocolats.

◄ 6.14 ►
Audio exercise

On the recording, answer the same questions from Exercise 6.12 in the negative. Pay close attention to the negative partitive.

EXAMPLE

PROMPT   Est-ce que tu vas visiter le Louvre?

RESPONSE   Non, je ne vais pas visiter le Louvre.

◄ 6.15 ►
Audio exercise

Using the vocabulary you have just learned, listen to the recording, and order a three-course meal. Tell the waiter what you want, following the prompts in English. Then, repeat the correct response after the speaker.

EXAMPLE

PROMPT   Qu'est-ce que vous voulez comme hors-d'œuvre?
          Une assiette de crudités, de la soupe à l'oignon ou
          des crevettes? (Onion soup, please.)

RESPONSE   De la soupe à l'oignon, s'il vous plaît.

◄ 6.16 ►
Exercise

Complete the following paragraph, using the correct form of the partitive: **du, de la, de l', des,** or **de**.

Au quartier Latin il y a _____ restaurants et _____

cafés-terrasse. Vous pouvez, si vous voulez, commander

_____ spécialités françaises, _____ café, _____ thé

ou _____ boissons. Si vous êtes gourmand (*food-loving*),

vous pouvez manger _____ glace à la framboise, _____

crêpes, _____ pêche Melba, _____ jus de pamplemousse,

mais vous ne pouvez pas avoir _____ spécialités mexicaines

ou brésiliennes dans un café français traditionnel.

◀ **6.17** ▶
DIALOGUE 3
Et pour finir! · *And for dessert!*

Our friends are finishing the meal.

Nos amis finissent le repas.

LE SERVEUR	Et pour finir?
M. JONES	Finir quoi?
LE SERVEUR	Finir le repas: c'est-à-dire, le dessert.
JENNIFER	Je ne veux pas de dessert, merci.
M. JONES	Moi non plus, mais je voudrais du café.
JEREMY	Qu'est-ce que c'est « la poire Belle Hélène »?
LE SERVEUR	C'est de la poire en compote, c'est-à-dire une compote de poire avec de la crème glacée.
JEREMY	Je choisis ça.
M. JONES	Nous voulons aussi l'addition, s'il vous plaît!

◀ **6.18** ▶
Petit lexique

ça	*it, that*
c'est-à-dire	*that is to say*
choisir	*to choose*
la compote	*compote*
en compote	*crushed (to pulp) (fruit)*
finir	*to finish*
glacé(e)	*icy; iced*
non plus	*neither*
la poire	*pear*
quoi	*what*
le repas	*meal*

◄ 6.19 ►
Compréhension et expressions

Pour finir

Pour finir simply means "to end," "to finish." You will often hear this expression in a French restaurant when the patron is being asked whether he/she wants dessert or coffee to end the meal. Similarly, you will also hear **pour commencer**, which suggests a choice of an appetizer.

Finir quoi? literally means "Finish what?"

Non plus

Moi non plus · *Neither do I*

In this expression, the stressed pronoun **moi** is followed by **non plus**, which means "neither."

Jeremy ne parle pas espagnol et M. Jones **non plus**.	*Jeremy does not speak Spanish, and neither does Mr. Jones.*
Je n'habite pas sur la lune et **vous non plus**.	*I don't live on the moon, and you don't either.*

◄ 6.20 ►
Structure grammaticale

Verbes réguliers en -*ir* · *Regular* -ir *verbs*

Like regular -**er** verbs, the -**ir** verbs have their own conjugation forms. Here are the endings, followed by examples of the verb **finir** ("to finish").

je	**-is**	nous	**-issons**
tu	**-is**	vous	**-issez**
il/elle/on	**-it**	ils/elles	**-issent**

Je **finis** le travail à six heures.	*I finish/am finishing work at 6 P.M.*
Tu **finis** le repas.	*You are finishing the meal.*
Elle **finit** le repassage.	*She is finishing the ironing.*
Nous **finissons** les devoirs.	*We are finishing the homework.*
Vous **finissez** l'apéritif.	*You are finishing the aperitif.*
Ils **finissent** la course.	*They are finishing the race.*

Here are some common -**ir** verbs.

avertir	*to warn*
choisir	*to choose*
grandir	*to grow*
grossir	*to gain weight*
maigrir	*to lose weight*
obéir (à)	*to obey*
punir	*to punish*
réfléchir (à)	*to ponder*
remplir	*to fill*
réussir	*to succeed*

◄ **6.21** ►
Audio exercise

Answer the questions on the recording in the affirmative, using -**ir** verbs.

EXAMPLE

PROMPT   Est-ce que vous choisissez un apéritif?
RESPONSE   Oui, je choisis un apéritif.

◄ **6.22** ►
Audio exercise

Answer the questions on the recording in the affirmative, using **aussi** in your answer.

EXAMPLE

PROMPT   M. Jones finit le repas. Et vous?
RESPONSE   Je finis le repas aussi.

◄ **6.23** ►
Exercise

Complete the following fairy tale with the correct form of the verb in parentheses.

Alice _____ (être) une petite fille qui

n'_____ pas (obéir). Elle _____ (décider)

de visiter le pays des Merveilles (*Wonderland*). Elle

_____ (rencontrer) deux lapins qui

_____ (bâtir) une maison (*house*) en sucre dans un

jardin (*garden*) magique. Dans le jardin, il y a aussi des fleurs

en chocolat. Les lapins _____ (inviter) Alice à entrer.

Elle _____ (prendre) un grand panier. Alice et les

deux lapins _____ (choisir) les chocolats et ils

_____ (remplir) le panier.

◄ 6.24 ►
Structure grammaticale
Verbes irréguliers en *-ir* · *Irregular -ir verbs*

Not all **-ir** verbs are regular; some verbs like **partir** ("to leave"), **dormir** ("to sleep"), **sortir** ("to go out"), and **servir** ("to serve") follow an irregular pattern of conjugation. Study the following conjugations and their example sentences.

PARTIR ("to leave")

je **pars**	Je **pars** en France.
tu **pars**	Tu **pars** au théâtre.
il/elle/on **part**	Il **part** en train à Dijon.
nous **partons**	Nous **partons** à deux heures.
vous **partez**	Vous ne **partez** pas au Maroc.
ils/elles **partent**	Elles **partent** au jardin du Luxembourg.

SERVIR ("to serve")

je **sers**	Je **sers** un café à Marie-Claire.
tu **sers**	Tu **sers** un apéritif avant le repas.
il/elle/on **sert**	On ne **sert** pas de salade avec la soupe en France.
nous **servons**	Nous **servons** du vin blanc avec du poisson.
vous **servez**	Vous **servez** les invités.
ils/elles **servent**	Elles **servent** les clients.

SORTIR ("to leave/to go out/to go out on a date")

je **sors**	Je **sors** de la maison.
tu **sors**	Tu **sors** avec Marie.
elle/il/on **sort**	Elle **sort** avec ses amis.

nous **sortons**　Sortons-nous ce soir?
vous **sortez**　Vous ne **sortez** pas le week-end?
ils/elles **sortent**　Ils **sortent** après la classe.

DORMIR ("to sleep")

je **dors**　Je ne **dors** pas en classe.
tu **dors**　Tu **dors** beaucoup?
il/elle/on **dort**　On **dort** à huit heures.
nous **dormons**　Nous ne **dormons** pas au cinéma.
vous **dormez**　Vous **dormez** dans un lit.
ils/elles **dorment**　Ils **dorment** tard le dimanche.
　　　　(tard, *late*)

 ◄ **6.25** ►
Audio exercise

The speaker on the recording will give you a sentence in English; translate it into French, using the irregular verbs you have just learned (**dormir**, **partir**, **sortir**, and **servir**). Then, repeat the correct response after the speaker.

EXAMPLE

PROMPT　I sleep a lot.
RESPONSE　Je dors beaucoup.

◄ **6.26** ►
Exercise

Select the appropriate verb (**partir**, **dormir**, **servir**, **sortir**), and complete the following paragraph with the correct verb forms.

Le week-end, je _____ avec Isabelle. Nous

_____ à huit heures du matin pour aller à la

campagne (*countryside*). Nous _____ en train jusqu'à

Chartres. En général, Isabelle _____ dans le train,

car elle aime dormir. Quand nous arrivons à Chartres, nous

_____ de la gare (*station*) pour aller déjeuner dans

un petit café. Isabelle veut commander une pizza; le garçon dit

—Je suis désolé, nous ne _____ pas de pizza, mais

on _____ des croque-monsieur.

◄ 6.27 ►
Common pitfalls

On the recording, listen to the class interaction between the student and the teacher. The student and the teacher are role-playing a scene in a restaurant, where the student is the customer and the teacher is the waiter.

This scene illustrates the importance of the preposition in French. It can change the entire meaning of an action verb. The same applies in English, as with "to look," "to look *for*," "to look *after*," "to look *up*," etc.

In this interaction, the teacher needs to explain the difference between **un verre** *de* **vin** ("a glass of wine," "a glass full of wine") and **un verre** *à* **vin** ("a glass for wine," "a wine glass"), which was what the student was trying to ask for.

◄ 6.28 ►
Let's take a plunge!

This exercise will test your aural comprehension skills as we take a deeper plunge into French. On the recording, listen to the speaker talking about various regions of France; then answer out loud the questions that follow.

Don't worry if you cannot understand every single word you hear; just try to get the gist of what is being said. However, here are some words you might need in order to understand the story.

célèbre	*famous*
n'est plus à faire	*need not be made/drawn*
mondial(e)	*worldwide*
la renommée	*reputation*

◄ 6.29 ►
Vive la différence!

L'apéritif

For the French the **apéritif** is a social affair. It is most often served before an elaborate meal. Some **apéritifs** have a wine and brandy base (for example, Byrrh and Dubonnet), while others have an **anise** ("licorice") base (for example, Pernod and Ricard).

Remember that drinks are more expensive if you sit at a table or outside on the terrace rather than at the bar or counter.

One of the most popular aperitifs is **Kir**, a mixture of white wine or, for **Kir royal**, champagne, with blackcurrant liqueur. It is named after a Catholic priest, Félix Kir, who became mayor of Dijon in the early 1960s.

Champagne

"Come quickly," Dom Pérignon called to the other monks, "I am tasting stars." And so the magical taste of champagne was created by the Benedictine monk in the seventeenth century.

Le champagne, the wine, bears the name of **La Champagne**, the region of France ninety miles northeast of Paris where it is made. By law, **le champagne** may be produced only within strictly limited boundaries, only from certain grape varieties, and only according to the **méthode champenoise**. Sparkling wines produced elsewhere in France are labeled **vin mousseux**.

There are four types of champagne:

Brut: the driest, which contains no sugar
Extra sec: extra dry with a hint of sweetness
Sec: dry but fairly sweet
Demi sec or **doux**: very sweet and suitable for dessert

French table manners

Like most Europeans, the French hold the fork in their left hand all the time, to secure the food while cutting with the knife, which is held in the right hand, and to bring the food to their mouth. They never switch the fork to the right hand after cutting their food, as many Americans tend to do.

During the meal, when the hands are not being used, they are never placed under the table. The wrists are kept on the edge of the table. This is left over from medieval times, when people may have feared the sudden use of a dagger hidden beneath the table.

◀ 6.30 ▶
How to make it sound French

Most consonants are not pronounced when they are the last letter of a word:

comment	salut	beaucoup	mais
entièrement	d'accord	français	Bordeaux

A single **s** is generally pronounced as /z/ between two vowels. For example, in a restaurant, at the end of a meal you should ask for **un dessert**, not **un désert**, which is pronounced /dezert/. Likewise, you would want to order some **poisson** ("fish"), not **poison**, pronounced as /poizon/.

◀ 6.31 ▶
Activities

To mark the completion of chapters 4 through 6, try the following activities.

A. Can you match the city or region with its specialty?

Cambrai	Bourgogne	Normandie	Cognac
Strasbourg	Dijon	Toulouse	Montélimar

LES SPÉCIALITÉS	LES VILLES ET PROVINCES
1. le nougat	_____
2. la moutarde	_____
3. la choucroute	_____
4. le Calvados	_____
5. Courvoisier	_____
6. les bêtises (*mint hard candy*)	_____
7. le cassoulet (*white beans and sausage stew*)	_____
8. le vin	_____

B. Voici quelques noms et mots masculins. Pouvez-vous donner le féminin?

1. un docteur   _____

2. un neveu   _____

3. un frère   _____

4. un Algérien   _____

5. un gendre   _____

6. un président   _____

7. un Français   _____

8. rapide   _____

9. messieurs   _____

10. fils   _____

La visite de Paris
Touring Paris

OBJECTIVE

In this chapter, you'll visit Paris and decide what to see! Of course, you must not miss the historic monuments, but what about other sites and districts? You will not get lost in French buildings, since you are learning to understand how floors are designated. Your knowledge of French continues to expand, so talk to the Parisians! Stay safe; this is a big city! You will also learn to use the possessive adjectives.

◄ **7.1** ►

DIALOGUE 1
Une décision difficile · *A hard decision*

The three "J"s have finished lunch, and they are going sightseeing in Paris. Jeremy wants to go straight to Pigalle, but Jennifer and Mr. Jones want to go to the Louvre.

Nos trois amis ont fini de déjeuner et ils veulent visiter Paris. Jeremy veut aller directement à Pigalle, mais Jennifer et M. Jones veulent aller au Louvre.

JEREMY	Prenons le métro pour aller à Pigalle!
JENNIFER	Non, attends, je veux voir la Joconde!
JEREMY	Tu veux voir la Jo-quoi?
JENNIFER	La Joconde de Léonard de Vinci!
M. JONES	La Mona Lisa!
JEREMY	Moi, je veux voir Pigalle.
M. JONES	Pigalle? Qu'est-ce qu'y a à voir à Pigalle?
JEREMY	Le Moulin Rouge...
JENNIFER	... et les Folies Bergère! On peut aussi entendre de la musique dans la rue.
M. JONES	Ah! La jeunesse! Ben nous, nous allons visiter le Louvre.
JENNIFER	Et toi, tu peux aller à Pigalle. Il est deux heures et demie. Rendez-vous devant la Pyramide à cinq heures moins le quart.

◄ **7.2** ►
Petit lexique

attendre	*to wait for*
ben (*slang for* bien)	*well*
la décision	*decision*
difficile	*difficult*
entendre	*to hear*
la jeunesse	*youth*
le métro	*subway*
la musique	*music*
qu'est-ce qui y'a?	*what is there?*
le rendez-vous	*appointment; meeting, date*
la rue	*street*
voir	*to see*

◄ 7.3 ►
Compréhension et expressions

Qu'est-ce qu'y a à voir? · *What's there to see?*

Notice in this expression the contraction **y a**, which stands for **il y a** ("there is," "there are"). Contractions are common in spoken French, just as in English. You have already seen **ça va** (for **cela va**) and **comme ci comme ça** (for **comme ceci, comme cela**).

◄ 7.4 ►
Structure grammaticale

Verbes réguliers en *-re* · *Regular -re verbs*

In the last dialogue, Jennifer tells Jeremy, **Non, attends, je veux voir la Joconde!** ("No, wait, I want to see the Mona Lisa!").

Attends is the imperative form of the verb **attendre**. Like regular **-er** and **-ir** verbs, the **-re** verbs have their own conjugation. Here are the **-re** endings in the present tense.

ATTENDRE ("to wait for")

j'attend-**s**	nous attend-**ons**
tu attend-**s**	vous attend-**ez**
il/elle/on attend_	ils/elles attend-**ent**

J'**attends** l'avion.	*I'm waiting for the plane.*
Tu **attends** la fin de la classe.	*You're waiting for the class to end.*
On **attend** l'arrivée du président.	*We are waiting for the arrival of the president.*
Nous **attendons** des amis.	*We are waiting for friends.*
Vous **attendez** un invité.	*You are waiting for a guest.*
Ils **attendent** les vacances.	*They are waiting for vacation.*

Here are some common **-re** verbs.

descendre	*to go down, to come down*
perdre	*to lose*
prétendre	*to claim*
rendre	*to give back, to return*
répondre	*to answer*
vendre	*to sell*

◄ 7.5 ►
Audio exercise

Answer the speaker's questions according to the sounds you hear on the recording, using the verb **entendre**. Then, repeat the correct answer after the speaker.

EXAMPLE

PROMPT   Cocorico! [rooster sound] (nous)
RESPONSE   Nous entendons le coq!

◄ 7.6 ►
Audio exercise

Listen to the mini-dictation on the recording. Repeat the sentences out loud, then complete the following sentences.

1. Nous _____ l'arrivée de nos amis.

2. Il _____ le passeport.

3. Pardon, Monsieur, _____-vous des télécartes?

4. Elle _____ les livres à la bibliothèque.
   (la bibliothèque, *library*)

5. On ne _____ pas en anglais aux questions!

6. Elles _____ être françaises.

◄ 7.7 ►
Exercise

Complete the following sentences with the appropriate form of the verb, selected from the following.

attendre   perdre   rendre   vendre
entendre   prétendre   répondre

1. Elle _____ avoir trente ans.

2. En quelle langue _____-vous au professeur?

3. _____-vous la sirène de la police?

4. Les amis _____ le serveur pour commander.

5. En France, on _____ des cigarettes au bar.

6. Nous _____ du temps à regarder la télévision.

◄ 7.8 ►
DIALOGUE 2
Au Louvre · *At the Louvre*

Mr. Jones and Jennifer are now at the Louvre. Let's listen to their conversation with the guide.

Jennifer et M. Jones sont maintenant au Louvre. Écoutons-les parler avec le guide.

JENNIFER	La Joconde, Monsieur, s'il vous plaît?
LE GUIDE	Galerie Richelieu, au premier étage au fond du couloir à gauche.
M. JONES	Et la Vénus de Milo, s'il vous plaît?
LE GUIDE	Ça c'est au rez-de-chaussée. Tout droit, et à votre droite.
JENNIFER ET M. JONES	Merci, Monsieur.
LE GUIDE	À votre service, Messieurs-dames.

(Devant la Joconde)

M. JONES	Elle, elle est belle.
JENNIFER	Moi, je pense qu'elle ressemble à mon ami Henry.

Remember to listen again to the dialogue, and repeat after each speaker.

◄ 7.9 ►
Petit lexique

le couloir	*corridor, hall*
droit(e)	*straight*
à droite	*to the right*
l'étage (*m.*)	*floor*
le fond	*back, far end*
à gauche	*to the left*
penser	*to think*
ressembler à	*to look like*
le rez-de-chaussée	*ground floor*
le service	*service, duty*
à votre service	*you are welcome*
tout droit	*straight ahead*

◄ 7.10 ►
Compréhension et expressions

C'est à quel étage?   ·   *What floor is it on?*

Floor numbering in France and in Europe does not correspond to the American system. When the French say **le rez-de-
chaussée**, they mean "ground floor," which Americans call the
"first floor." Continuing upward, **le premier étage** becomes "the
second floor," **le deuxième étage** becomes "the third floor," and
so on.

Les nombres ordinaux   ·   *Ordinal numbers*

troisième étage
quatrième étage
cinquième étage
sixième étage
septième étage
huitième étage
neuvième étage
dixième étage

Les directions

à gauche   *to the left*
à droite   *to the right*
tout droit   *straight ahead*

À votre service means "you're welcome."

◄ **7.11** ►
Audio exercise

You are in the Galeries Lafayette in Paris, and you are giving directions to the customers who appear on the recording. Look at the floor indications below, and tell the customer where to go. Then, repeat the correct answer after the speaker.

EXAMPLE

```
◄10► Musique
 ◄9► Jeux et jouets
 ◄8► Chaussures, Mode homme
 ◄7► Souvenirs de Paris
 ◄6► Électroménager
 ◄5► Chocolats, Porcelaine de Limoges
 ◄4► Livres
 ◄3► Mode enfant
 ◄2► Mode femme, Lingerie
 ◄1► Parfums
 ◄0► Sport
```

PROMPT   S'il vous plaît, les parfums, c'est à quel étage?
RESPONSE C'est au premier étage.

◄ **7.12** ►
Structure grammaticale

Singulier des adjectifs possessifs · *Singular form of the possessive adjectives*

In French, possession and relationship are expressed with **de**, while in English "'s" is typically added to the end of the word.

Jeremy est l'ami **de** Jennifer.   *Jeremy is Jennifer's friend.*
Les parents **de** Jennifer sont   *Jennifer's parents are*
   américains.   *American.*

While in English the possessive adjective ("my, your, his, her, our, their") agrees with the subject of the sentence or the possessor, the reverse happens in French. In French, the possessive adjective agrees in gender (masculine or feminine) and in number (singular or plural) with the object or thing that is possessed (the noun that follows).

Singular form of the possessive

If there is only one possessor and the object (the following noun) is masculine singular:

> **mon** ("my")   **mon** père
> **ton** ("your")   **ton** père
> **son** ("his/her")   **son** père

If there is only one possessor and the object (the following noun) is feminine singular:

> **ma** ("my")   **ma** mère
> **ta** ("your")   **ta** mère
> **sa** ("his/her")   **sa** mère

NOTE: The same possessive adjective is used whether it is Jennifer or Jeremy speaking of her or his father: Jennifer will say *mon* **père**, and Jeremy will say *mon* **père**.

Likewise, when either of them is speaking of her or his mother, Jennifer will say *ma* **mère**, and Jeremy will say *ma* **mère**.

If the noun starts with a vowel or silent **h**, even if it is feminine, we use the masculine form of the possessive adjective (**mon/ton/son**).

> Marie-France, c'est **mon** amie.

◄ 7.13 ►
Exercise

Answer the following questions in the affirmative, using the possessive adjective.

EXAMPLE   Est-ce que ta mère est journaliste?
     Oui, ma mère est journaliste.

1. Jennifer, est-ce que ton père parle français?

_____

2. Jeremy, est-ce que ta mère parle anglais?

_____

3. Est-ce que le père de Jennifer est américain?

_____

4. Est-ce que la mère de Jeremy est américaine?

_____

5. Est-ce que Marie-France est la petite amie de Jeremy?

_____

6. Est-ce que c'est le stylo de la réceptionniste?

_____

 ◄ 7.14 ►
DIALOGUE 3
À Pigalle · _In the Pigalle district_

Jeremy is visiting Pigalle, the famous entertainment district in Paris.

Jeremy visite Pigalle, le quartier parisien des spectacles.

JEREMY   Le Moulin Rouge, s'il vous plaît?

PASSANTE   Ah, Monsieur, c'est derrière vous. Vous allez dans la
           mauvaise direction. C'est à côté du nouveau cinéma
           le Colisée et en face de la vieille fontaine Pigalle.
           Mais, c'est relâche en juillet.

JEREMY   « Relâche, » c'est un beau spectacle?

PASSANTE   Il n'y a rien à voir.

JEREMY   Vous n'aimez pas le spectacle « Relâche »?

PASSANTE   Mais mon bon Monsieur vous ne voyez pas que tous
           les théâtres sont fermés; leurs portes sont fermées.
           « Relâche » veut dire fermé, en congé.

◄ 7.15 ►
Petit lexique

le congé	_leave, time off_
dire	_to tell; to say_
fermé(e)	_closed_
leur (_pl._ leurs)	_their_

mauvais(e)	*bad; wrong*
ouvert(e)	*open*
le passant/la passante	*passerby*
la relâche	*break, no performance*
rien	*nothing*
le spectacle	*show; sight*
tout (*pl.* tous)	*all, every*
vieux/vieille	*old*
vouloir dire	*to mean*

Extension de vocabulaire

la famille	*family*
les parents (*m.pl.*)	*parents; relatives*
le père	*father*
la mère	*mother*
le mari	*husband*
la femme	*wife; woman*
les enfants (*m.pl.*)	*children*
le fils	*son*
la fille	*daughter*
le frère	*brother*
la sœur	*sister*
le demi-frère	*stepbrother; half brother*
la demi-sœur	*stepsister; half sister*
les grands-parents (*m.pl.*)	*grandparents*
le grand-père	*grandfather*
la grand-mère	*grandmother*
le petit-fils	*grandson*
la petite-fille	*granddaughter*
l'oncle (*m.*)	*uncle*
la tante	*aunt*
le cousin/la cousine	*cousin*
le neveu	*nephew*
la nièce	*niece*
les beaux-parents (*m.pl.*)	*parents-in-law*
le beau-père	*father-in-law*
la belle-mère	*mother-in-law*
le beau-frère	*brother-in-law*
la belle-sœur	*sister-in-law*

◀ 7.16 ▶
Compréhension et expressions

Relâche · *No performance*

When Jeremy asks the woman in the street about the Moulin Rouge, she tells him, **C'est relâche en juillet. Relâche (faire relâche)** means "no performance today" for a theater or a movie house.

She goes on to tell him that **relâche** means **fermé, en congé.** The term **être en congé** means "to be off," "to be on leave."

◀ 7.17 ▶
Structure grammaticale

Pluriel des adjectifs possessifs · *Plural form of the possessive adjectives*

If there are several possessors and the object (the following noun) is singular (masculine or feminine), use the following forms.

notre ("our")	**notre** père, **notre** mère
votre ("your")	**votre** père, **votre** mère
leur ("their")	**leur** père, **leur** mère

If there is only one possessor and the object (the following noun) is plural (masculine or feminine), use the following forms.

mes ("my")	**mes** amis, **mes** amies
tes ("your")	**tes** amis, **tes** amies
ses ("his/her")	**ses** amis, **ses** amies

If there are several possessors and the object (the following noun) is plural (masculine or feminine), use the following forms.

nos ("our")	**nos** beaux-parents, **nos** belles-mères
vos ("your")	**vos** cousins, **vos** cousines
leurs ("their")	**leurs** neveux, **leurs** nièces

◀ 7.18 ▶
Audio exercise

Answer the questions on the recording in the affirmative, using a possessive adjective. Then, repeat the correct answer after the speaker.

EXAMPLE

PROMPT   Le père de Jennifer est docteur?
RESPONSE Oui, son père est docteur.

◄ 7.19 ►
Exercise

Complete the following sentences with the correct form of the possessive adjectives: **mon, ma, mes, ton, ta, tes, son, sa, ses, notre, votre, leur, nos, vos, leurs.**

1. M. Jones est divorcé. _____ ex-femme et _____ enfants ne sont pas en France avec lui.

2. Les parents adorent _____ enfants.

3. M. et Mme Boulanger vont vendre _____ maison.

4. Je mange toujours _____ salade après le plat principal.

5. Ton père est australien, et _____ mère?

6. Que faites-vous avec _____ stylo?

7. Avez-vous des problèmes avec votre télévision?

   Oui, _____ télévision ne marche pas.

8. Aimez-vous _____ belle-mère?

◄ 7.20 ►
Structure grammaticale

Verbes irréguliers · *Irregular verbs*

Voir ("to see") and **boire** ("to drink") have very similar singular present-tense conjugation forms.

VOIR	BOIRE
je vois	je bois
tu vois	tu bois
il/elle/on voit	il/elle/on boit

Je vois le Sacré-Cœur de mon hôtel.	*I can see the Sacré-Coeur from my hotel.*
Je bois du jus d'orange le matin.	*I drink orange juice in the morning.*

Tu vois le train qui arrive?	*Can you see the train that is arriving?*
Tu bois un verre de vin avec le déjeuner.	*You drink a glass of wine with lunch.*
On ne voit pas la lune le jour.	*You can't see the moon during the day.*
Elle boit du champagne pour son anniversaire.	*She drinks champagne on her birthday.*

However, the forms vary in the plural.

nous voyons	nous buvons
vous voyez	vous buvez
ils/elles voient	ils/elles boivent

Nous voyons la Seine.	*We see the Seine.*
Nous buvons du café à la terrasse des Deux Magots.	*We are drinking coffee on the terrace of the Deux Magots.*
Voyez-vous le jardin du Luxembourg de votre hôtel?	*Can you see the Luxembourg garden from your hotel?*
Buvez-vous de l'eau pétillante?	*Are you drinking/Do you drink carbonated water?*
Ils ne voient pas souvent leurs beaux-parents.	*They don't see their in-laws often.*
Elles ne boivent pas d'apéritif.	*They are not drinking/ don't drink aperitifs.*

 ◄ 7.21 ►
Audio exercise

Answer the questions on the recording in the negative. Then, repeat the correct answer after the speaker.

EXAMPLE

PROMPT   Est-ce que tu bois du champagne au petit déjeuner?

RESPONSE   Non, je ne bois pas de champagne au petit déjeuner.

◄ 7.22 ►
Exercise

Complete the following sentences with the correct form of **voir** or **boire**.

1. Pour le Nouvel An, les Français _____ du champagne toute la nuit.

2. Le grand-père de Jeremy a quatre-vingt-dix ans, il ne _____ pas bien.

3. Les touristes adorent _____ les monuments historiques.

4. On ne _____ pas sur l'autoroute. (l'autoroute (*f.*), *highway*)

5. Les enfants aiment _____ le soda.

6. En Normandie, nous _____ du cidre.

7. On _____ l'Obélisque sur la place de la Concorde.

8. Elles _____ Gérard Depardieu dans un film.

◄ 7.23 ►
Common pitfalls

Listen to the following class interaction between the student and the teacher on the recording. The teacher and the student meet unexpectedly at the train station (**à la gare**).

Many students have a tendency to mistakenly use the verb **attendre** ("to wait for") for the verb **entendre** ("to hear"). As in this case, they also often mistake it for its English false cognate "to attend," which in French is translated by the verb **aller à/au/à la**.

Jennifer va à l'université means Jennifer is "going to" school or Jennifer "attends" school, but **Jennifer va à la maison/ au restaurant** simply means Jennifer is "going home/to the restaurant."

◄ 7.24 ►
Let's take a plunge!

Now you are going to test your aural comprehension skills, as we prepare to take a deeper plunge into French. Listen to the funny story (**histoire drôle**) on the recording, then answer out loud the questions that you hear.

Again, don't worry if you cannot understand every single word you hear. Try to get the gist of things!

Here are some words you might need to understand the story. Study them first!

a-t-il fallu?	*did it take?, did it require?*
construire	*to build*
la cathédrale	*cathedral*
n'était pas ici	*was not here*
hier	*yesterday*
le pays	*country*
plus tard	*later*
se promener	*to stroll, to walk leisurely*

◄ 7.25 ►
Vive la différence!

The Louvre

Le Louvre, built around 1200, was originally a fortress, a tower, and a keep surrounded by a thick wall. It became the royal residence with Charles V in 1360, and remained so until Louis XIV moved his residence to Versailles. During the French Revolution, in 1793, the Louvre was opened to the "people" and turned into a museum.

The Louvre's wealth is due mostly to the kings of France. Among them, François I stands out for bringing back from Italy not only the famous Mona Lisa but also the artist himself, Leonardo da Vinci, who spent the last years of his life in France. The French call the Mona Lisa **La Joconde**, and her mysterious smile continues to attract millions of visitors every year.

◄ 7.26 ►
How to make it sound French

The **é** sound is pronounced with words ending in:

-ez	chez /ché/, rez-de-chaussée /ré-de-chaussée/
-er	réserver /réservé/, manger /mangé/

É is also the sound of **et** ("and").

◄ *8* ►

Randonnée à travers la France
Roaming across France

OBJECTIVE

In this chapter, even though you love Paris, you are making plans to see the provinces. You go to a travel agency to make reservations for the TGV (**Train à Grande Vitesse**, "high-speed train") to visit the famous prehistoric caves of Lascaux, as well as the Burgundy region. Once you get there, you will need to rent a car. You will also learn to express yourself using the past tense.

◄ 8.1 ►
DIALOGUE 1
À l'agence de voyages · *At the travel agency*

Our friends wish to visit the famous prehistoric caves of Lascaux in the southwest of France, near Bordeaux. They go to a travel agency to make arrangements.

Nos trois amis veulent visiter les grottes préhistoriques de Lascaux dans le sud-ouest de la France, près de Bordeaux. Ils se rendent dans une agence de voyages pour faire les préparatifs.

L'AGENT	Bonjour, vous désirez?
JEREMY	Nous voulons visiter la préhistoire.
L'AGENT	Pour la préhistoire, Monsieur, vous devez aller au musée du Louvre.
M. JONES	Mais qu'est-ce qu'ils ont ces Parisiens, ils ne parlent pas français!
JENNIFER	Non, Monsieur, pas le Louvre, les caves de la préhistoire.
L'AGENT	Les caves à vin, ça je connais, mais je ne sais pas où sont les caves de la préhistoire.
JENNIFER	Pas les caves à vin, Monsieur, les caves de la préhistoire en Dordogne.
L'AGENT	Ah, vous voulez visiter les grottes de Lascaux. D'accord. Donc, vous devez passer par Bordeaux.
M. JONES	Bordeaux?
L'AGENT	Oui, Bordeaux et ensuite louer une voiture jusqu'en Dordogne.
JENNIFER	Et comment aller dans cette région?
L'AGENT	Vous avez deux possibilités; vous pouvez prendre l'avion ou le TGV.
JEREMY	Ce TGV, qu'est-ce que c'est?
L'AGENT	C'est le train à grande vitesse; c'est rapide et économique.

Listen again to the dialogue, and repeat after the speaker.

◄ 8.2 ►
Petit lexique

l'agence de voyages (f.)	*travel agency*
la cave	*cellar, basement*
la cave à vin	*wine cellar*
ces	*these, those*

comment	*how*
donc	*therefore*
connaître	*to know*
la grotte	*cave, cavern*
jusque	*as far as*
louer	*to rent*
passer par	*to go through*
la possibilité	*possibility*
la préhistoire	*prehistory*
la randonnée	*excursion*
rapide	*fast*
la région	*region, area*
à travers	*through*
la vitesse	*speed*
la voiture	*car*

◄ **8.3** ►
Compréhension et expressions
Caves/grottes

Jennifer seems to be having trouble with the travel agent. Indeed, when she asks for **les caves de la préhistoire**, she is using a **faux ami** for English "cave," which in French means a place underground (a cellar) where wine or cheese is aged. What she should have said is **les grottes**.

passer par · *to go through*

The travel agent says, **Vous devez passer par Bordeaux**. The expression **passer par** means literally "to go by" or, more properly, "to go through." The appropriate meaning in English will vary according to context.

La Seine **passe par** Paris.	*The Seine **runs through** Paris.*
Le train **passe par** Dijon.	*The train **goes via** Dijon.*

◄ **8.4** ►
Exercise

Répondez à ces questions qui portent sur le dialogue.

1. Qu'est-ce que les amis veulent visiter?

    _____

2. L'agent ne comprend pas; pourquoi?

    _____

3. Où sont les grottes?

    _____

4. Par où doit-on passer pour aller aux grottes?

    _____

5. Qu'est-ce qu'on doit louer pour aller en Dordogne?

    _____

6. Quelles sont les deux possibilités pour aller à Bordeaux?

    _____

7. Le TGV, c'est quoi?

    _____

◄ **8.5** ►
Structure grammaticale

Les démonstratifs · *Demonstratives*

Demonstrative adjectives ("this, that, these, those") are used to point out or to help focus on a person or a thing in a sentence. In the dialogue above, we encountered the following examples.

Qu'est-ce qu'ils ont **ces** Parisiens?	*What's the matter with these Parisians?*
Comment aller dans **cette** région?	*How do we get there? (literally, How do we go to this region?)*
Ce TGV, qu'est-ce que c'est?	*This TGV, what is it?*

Like all adjectives, the demonstratives agree in gender and number with the (following) noun they modify or qualify.

Singular · *this/that*

ce	ce garçon	*if the noun is masculine singular*
cet	cet homme	*if the noun is masculine singular and starts with a vowel or silent* **h**
cette	cette femme	*if the noun is feminine singular*

Plural · *these/those*

ces	ces garçons	*if the noun is masculine or feminine*
	ces hommes	*plural*
	ces femmes	

◄ 8.6 ►
Audio exercise

It's time to review the demonstratives and the stressed pronouns, first introduced in Chapter 4. Listen to the recording, and reword the sentences to incorporate the stressed pronoun, repeating the correct response after the speaker.

EXAMPLE

PROMPT   C'est mon livre!

RESPONSE   Ce livre est à moi!

◄ 8.7 ►
Exercise

Complete the following dialogue between Jennifer and her mother, using the demonstratives: **ce**, **cet**, **cette**, **ces**.

1. Maman, regarde _____ beau gâteau!

2. _____ tarte est plus belle.

3. Avec toutes _____ pâtisseries, adieu ton régime! (ton régime, *your diet*)

4. Tu as raison, ma chérie, mais _____ éclair, ce n'est pas beaucoup de calories.

5. Oublie tous _____ gâteaux et mange des fruits comme _____ homme à côté de toi. (oublier, *to forget*)

◄ **8.8** ►

DIALOGUE 2
Un aller et retour en TGV · *A round-trip ticket on the TGV*

Our friends are discussing the possibility of traveling to Bordeaux by TGV.

Nos amis discutent de leur voyage à Bordeaux en TGV avec le voyagiste.

L'AGENT	Vous avez décidé?
JEREMY	Oui, nous avons choisi le TGV.
L'AGENT	Alors, trois aller et retour en TGV. Quand voulez-vous partir?
M. JONES	Le 17 juillet.
L'AGENT	À quelle heure? Dans la matinée? Il y a un départ à 9 heures 28, un autre à 11 heures 46.
M. JONES	Nous préférons partir l'après-midi.
L'AGENT	Bien, Monsieur, il y a un départ à 14 heures 58.
JEREMY	14 heures 58, c'est quelle heure?
L'AGENT	14 heures 58, c'est trois heures moins deux minutes.
M. JONES, JEREMY ET JENNIFER	D'accord.
L'AGENT	Et le retour? Vous voulez des réservations ou des billets ouverts?
M. JONES	Des billets ouverts, s'il vous plaît, c'est combien?
L'AGENT	C'est 148 euros par personne. J'ai vendu beaucoup de billets ouverts cette semaine.

Listen again to the dialogue, and repeat after the speaker.

◄ **8.9** ►
Petit lexique

l'aller et retour (*m.*)	*round-trip ticket*
autre	*other*
le billet ouvert	*open ticket*
dans la matinée	*in the morning (during the morning hours)*
le départ	*departure*
le retour	*return*
le TGV (Train à Grande Vitesse)	*high-speed train*
le/la voyagiste	*travel agent*

◄ 8.10 ►
Compréhension et expressions

Les moments de la journée · *Times of the day*

Matinée

The travel agent says, **Dans la matinée, il y a un départ**. The word **matinée** is another word for **matin** or "morning" in French. It is a period of time between sunrise and noon. **Dans la matinée** means "in the morning."

Je dois aller au marché dans la matinée.	*I have to go to the market in the morning.*

Matinée can also mean an afternoon performance. The reason for this is that years ago, movie theaters had morning performances for French children on Thursdays.

À Broadway, il y a des matinées le mercredi après-midi.	*Broadway theaters offer matinee performances on Wednesdays.*

Soirée/journée

The principle for **matin/matinée** also applies to **soir** ("evening") and **soirée** ("period of time in the evening"), and **jour** ("a 24-hour day") and **journée** ("daylight hours").

NOTE: Do not mistake **journée** for the false cognate "journey."

Bonne journée!	*Have a good day!*
Ce soir, nous allons passer la soirée avec nos amis.	*This evening we are going to spend a couple of hours (the evening) with our friends.*

Aller et retour · *Round-trip*

The agent says **trois aller et retour en TGV**. This simply means a round-trip or return ticket. For a single or a one-way ticket, he would say **un aller simple**.

Finally, the travel agent asks, **Et le retour? Vous voulez des réservations ou des billets ouverts?** The term **billet ouvert** means an "open ticket," not reserved for a particular day or time.

Audio exercise

The speaker will ask you a question on the recording. You will be prompted in English; give the answer in French. Then, repeat the answer after the speaker.

EXAMPLE

PROMPT   C'est pour un aller simple ou un aller et retour?
    (A one-way ticket, please.)
RESPONSE   Un aller simple, s'il vous plaît.

◄ **8.12** ►
Structure grammaticale

Le passé composé des verbes réguliers · *Past tense of regular verbs*

To express events that happened in the past, French uses several different tenses. Probably the most common one is the **passé composé**. This is a compound tense formed by an auxiliary (helping) verb and a past participle.

Verbes conjugués avec *avoir*

Let's study again the conversation between Jeremy and the travel agent.

L'AGENT   Vous avez décidé?
JEREMY   Oui, nous avons choisi de prendre le TGV. Mais nous n'avons pas décidé la date de notre retour. Pouvons-nous avoir des billets ouverts?
L'AGENT   J'ai vendu dix billets ouverts dans la matinée, pas de problème.

The travel agent has asked Jeremy whether they had made up their minds. Jeremy answered in the affirmative, telling him that they had chosen open tickets. In this short dialogue, the agent and Jeremy are using the past tense, **passé composé**. Let's look at the structure of this tense.

vous avez décidé?	*we decided/we have decided*
nous avons choisi	*we chose/we have chosen*

nous n'avons pas décidé	*we haven't decided/we did not decide*
j'ai vendu	*I sold/I have sold*

Notice the presence of the auxiliary verb **avoir** and the past participle. In fact, most French verbs are conjugated with the present tense of the auxiliary **avoir**. These verbs are known as "verbs of action."

Formation of the past participle of regular verbs

INFINITIVE	PAST PARTICIPLE
-er verbs	*remove* **-er** *ending and add* **-é**
mang**er**	mangé
-ir verbs	*remove* **-ir** *ending and add* **-i**
fin**ir**	fini
-re verbs	*remove* **-re** *ending and add* **-u**
atten**dre**	atten**du**

For most irregular verbs, the past participle has its own special form that needs to be learned.

INFINITIVE	PAST PARTICIPLE
boire	**bu**
faire	**fait**
mettre	**mis**
prendre	**pris**
voir	**vu**

◄ 8.13 ►
Audio exercise

Listen to the questions on the recording, and answer in the affirmative. Then, repeat the correct answer after the speaker.

EXAMPLE

PROMPT Tu as mangé le sandwich?

RESPONSE Oui, j'ai mangé le sandwich.

◄ **8.14** ►
Audio exercise

Look at the pictures and describe out loud the action, using the past tense (**passé composé**) of the verb. Then, repeat the correct response after the speaker on the recording.

1. acheter

2. travailler

3. chanter

4. choisir

5. répondre

6. prendre

◄ **8.15** ►
Exercise

Complete the following sentences, using the **passé composé** form of the verb in parentheses.

1. J'_____ la télé avec mes amis. (regarder)

2. Tu _____ ton devoir de français. (finir)

3. Vous _____ le français. (apprendre)

4. Il _____ sa bicyclette. (vendre)

5. Ils _____ au téléphone? (parler)

6. Elle _____ un bon film. (choisir)

7. Marie-Paule et Marc _____ le départ de l'avion. (attendre)

8. Ils _____ la voiture au garage. (mettre)

9. Elle _____ une grande randonnée à travers la Dordogne. (faire)

10. On _____ une bouteille d'eau gazeuse. (boire)

◄ **8.16** ►
DIALOGUE 3
Location de voiture · *Car rental*

Our friends are still at the travel agency, where they discuss renting a car.

Nos amis sont toujours à l'agence de voyages. Ils veulent louer une voiture.

L'AGENT   Et la voiture, vous voulez faire la réservation maintenant?

M. JONES   Oui, s'il vous plaît, une voiture automatique.

JENNIFER   Surtout pas rouge, plutôt blanche.

JEREMY   Mais Jennifer, qu'est-ce que ça peut faire si elle est rouge, jaune, verte ou noire? L'important c'est d'avoir une voiture automatique.

L'AGENT   Je vais essayer de trouver une voiture automatique, car beaucoup de voitures françaises sont à embrayage. Bien, ça vous fait 190 euros.

M. JONES   Avez-vous compté le TGV?

L'AGENT   Non, c'est seulement pour la location de la voiture.
Vous allez payer avec votre carte de crédit à la gare de Bordeaux. Au revoir, Messieurs-dames et bonne journée.

Listen again to the dialogue, and repeat after the speaker.

◄ 8.17 ►
Petit lexique

blanc/blanche	*white*
bleu(e)	*blue*
car	*because*
la carte de crédit	*credit card*
l'embrayage (*m.*)	*clutch (car)*
l'important (*m.*)	*important thing*
la location	*rental*
maintenant	*now*
noir(e)	*black*
plutôt	*rather*
surtout	*especially, above all*
la voiture à embrayage	*car with manual transmission*
la voiture automatique	*car with automatic transmission*

◄ 8.18 ►
Compréhension et expressions

Location · *Rental*

The French word **location** means "rental." It can easily be mistaken for its false English cognate "location," which means "place."

The word **location** comes from the verb **louer** ("to rent").

Nous **louons** des bicyclettes dans le Bois de Boulogne.	*We rent/are renting bicycles in the Bois de Boulogne.*
Sur la Côte d'azur, il y a des maisons à **louer**.	*There are houses for rent on the Côte d'Azur.*
À l'aéroport, il y a des **bureaux de location** de voiture.	*There are car rental offices at the airport.*
Nos amis ont une **voiture de location** pour visiter la Dordogne.	*Our friends have a rental car to visit the Dordogne.*

L'important c'est de/d' + *infinitive* · *What is important/ essential is to* + infinitive

L'important, c'est de parler français à Paris.	*What is important is to speak French in Paris.*
L'important, c'est d'arriver à l'heure.	*The important thing is to arrive on time.*

Qu'est-ce que ça peut faire? · *What does it matter?*

This expression is generally followed by **si** (**si elle, s'il**). Jeremy says, **Qu'est-ce que ça peut faire *si* la voiture est rouge?**

Qu'est-ce que ça peut faire s'il pleut?	*What does it matter if it rains?*
Qu'est-ce que ça peut faire s'il ne parle pas espagnol?	*So what if he doesn't speak Spanish?*

Surtout pas... · *Especially not . . .*

Jennifer says, **Surtout pas rouge, plutôt blanche**. Jennifer does not want a red car.

◄ **8.19** ►

Structure grammaticale

Interrogation au passé composé · *Questions in the past tense*

In the dialogue above, Mr. Jones says, **Avez-vous compté le TGV?** ("Have you included the TGV?") Form the inversion of a question in the past tense by switching the auxiliary and the subject pronoun. In other words, instead of

subject pronoun + auxiliary + past participle

use

auxiliary + subject pronoun + past participle

Avez-vous réservé une table au restaurant?	*Did you reserve a table at the restaurant?*
As-tu choisi un bon film pour ce soir?	*Have you chosen a good movie for this evening?*

Ont-ils entendu la pluie?   *Did they hear the rain?*
A-t-elle répondu à la lettre   *Has she replied to her friend's*
   de son amie?   *letter?*

Negation au passé composé · *Negative sentences in the past tense*

In negative sentences in the past, the present tense of the auxiliary **avoir** is made negative.

Elle **n'**a **pas** payé avec sa   *She didn't pay with her credit*
   carte de crédit.   *card.*
Je **n'**ai **pas** fait la réservation. *I didn't make the reservation.*
Nous **n'**avons **pas** loué de   *We didn't rent a car in*
   voiture à Bordeaux.   *Bordeaux.*

◄ 8.20 ►
Audio exercise

Transform the statements on the recording into questions, using inversion. Then, repeat the correct response after the speaker.

EXAMPLE

PROMPT   Vous avez mangé des glaces au restaurant.
RESPONSE   Avez-vous mangé des glaces au restaurant?

◄ 8.21 ►
Audio exercise

Answer the speaker on the recording in the negative. Then, repeat the correct answer after the speaker.

EXAMPLE

PROMPT   Avez-vous commandé le dessert?
RESPONSE   Non, je n'ai pas commandé le dessert.

◄ 8.22 ►
Exercise

Complete the following sentences with one of the following verbs in the **passé composé**.

faire	attendre	écouter
vendre	choisir	visiter
prendre	acheter	louer

1. Elle _____ son appartement.

2. _____ vous _____ une voiture quand

    vous _____ la France?

3. Nous n'_____ pas _____ le discours
    du président. (le discours, *speech*)

4. J'_____ mes devoirs avant d'aller au
    cinéma.

5. Nous _____ le train pendant deux
    heures.

6. Elle _____ un Kir royal comme apéritif.

7. Ils _____ des billets ouverts.

8. _____-t-elle _____ à sa belle-mère?

◄ 8.23 ►
Common pitfalls

In the previous chapter, we saw that the system of floor designation in the United States is different from the one in Europe and elsewhere in the world. This can lead to rather amusing situations, as in the class interaction between the student and the teacher on the recording.

The student did not realize that what is commonly referred to as "the first floor" in the United States is known in France and elsewhere as the "ground floor," or **rez-de-chaussée**. Consequently, the second floor becomes **le premier étage** ("first floor"), the third floor **le deuxième étage** ("second floor"), and so on. So the student went to the second floor, thinking that he was on the third floor.

◄ **8.24** ►
Let's take a plunge!

Now you are going to test your aural comprehension skills as we prepare to take a real plunge into French. First, listen to a funny story (**histoire drôle**) on the recording, then answer out loud the questions the speaker asks you about it.

Don't worry if you cannot understand every single word you hear! Try to get the gist of things! Here are some words you might need to understand the story. Study them first!

aboyer	*to bark*
aujourd'hui	*today*
le chien	*dog*
étranger	*foreign*
miauler	*to meow*
rentrer	*to return; to come back*
savoir (je sais)	*to know (I know)*

◄ **8.25** ►
Vive la différence!

Trains

The railroad system was introduced in France in 1827, not long after it was established in Great Britain. By 1938, the French government had nationalized the system to form the S.N.C.F. (**Société Nationale des Chemins de Fer Français**). Today, despite modern air travel, the train is still unmatched as a way to travel around France.

How can this be? Probably because of the high-speed technology introduced in 1983 with the TGV (**Train à Grande Vitesse**, "high-speed train"). The French trains have a reputation for being a fast, punctual, and very efficient means of transportation. Cruising at speeds of over 250 miles per hour, the TGV continues to expand its routes and connections with the major cities of France and throughout Europe.

Compostez votre billet! You must stamp your ticket at one of the orange boxes at the platform entrance before boarding the train.

◄ 9 ►

Provinces de France
French provinces

OBJECTIVE

In this chapter, you will have adventures while visiting Dordogne and Burgundy and experiencing the flavor of these provinces. You prepare yourself for a glorious French picnic by buying fresh produce in the local stores. You continue to expand your ability to express yourself in the past tense. Perhaps, like Jeremy, you indulge yourself and sample too many different wines from Burgundy! You'll also memorize a poem, "Déjeuner du matin" by Jacques Prévert.

◄ 9.1 ►

DIALOGUE 1
Chez l'homme des cavernes · *Visiting prehistoric man*

Our three friends are in Lascaux, Dordogne. They are visiting the prehistoric caves . . . but where is Jeremy?

Nos trois amis sont à Lascaux. Ils visitent les grottes préhistoriques... mais où est Jeremy?

JENNIFER   Oh, j'ai peur!

M. JONES   Moi, j'ai froid. On ne voit pas Jeremy. Où est-il?

JENNIFER   Lui, il doit être dehors en train de manger son sandwich.

M. JONES   C'est vrai, lui, il a toujours faim!

JENNIFER   Chut, écoutez, qu'est-ce que c'est?

M. JONES   Je ne sais pas.

JENNIFER   Venez ici, vous allez mieux entendre.

M. JONES   Ah oui, j'entends marcher, c'est peut-être Monsieur de Cromagnon.

JENNIFER   Ou un brigand. Il vient dans cette direction. J'ai vraiment peur. Sortons vite!

JEREMY   Attendez, c'est moi. Venez par ici, il y a des stalactites magnifiques.

JENNIFER   Nous ne sommes pas ici pour faire de la spéléologie, mais pour voir les peintures rupestres.

JEREMY   Si, si, ça vaut le coup.

M. JONES   Non, une autre fois. Nous avons faim. Allons manger.

Listen again to the dialogue, then repeat each sentence after the speaker.

◄ 9.2 ►
Petit lexique

le brigand	*robber*
ça vaut le coup	*it is worth it*
la caverne	*cavern, cave*
Chut!	*Hush!*
la direction	*direction*
dehors	*outside*
être en train de	*to be in the act of*
magnifique	*magnificent*
la peinture	*painting*

la peinture rupestre	*rock painting*
peut-être	*perhaps, maybe*
préhistorique	*prehistoric*
le sandwich	*sandwich*
la spéléologie	*speleology, cave exploration*
la stalactite	*stalactite*
vraiment	*truly, really*

◄ 9.3 ►
Compréhension et expressions

en train de · *in the act of, in the process of*

This phrase expresses a continuous action, "in the process of doing something." It corresponds to the form of the verb ending in **-ing** in English.

—Allô, est-ce que je peux parler à Pierre?	*"Hello, may I speak with Pierre?"*
—Je suis désolé, il est **en train de** prendre sa douche.	*"Sorry, he's taking a shower."*

Ça vaut le coup de/d'..., Ça vaut la peine de/d'... · *It's worth it . . . , It's worth the hassle . . .*

Ça ne vaut pas la peine d'être stressé.	*It's not worth it to be stressed.*
Est-ce que ça vaut le coup de visiter les grottes de Lascaux?	*Is it worth visiting the caves at Lascaux?*

Notice that the verb following **de/d'** is in the infinitive.

◄ 9.4 ►
Audio exercise

The speaker will prompt you as to whether or not it is worth performing an action. Answer in French according to the prompt. Then, repeat the correct answer after the speaker.

EXAMPLE

PROMPT   Est-ce que ça vaut le coup de prendre le train?
         (It's quicker by plane.)
RESPONSE   Non, ça ne vaut pas le coup!

◄ **9.5** ►
Structure grammaticale

Verbe irrégulier *venir* · *Irregular verb* venir *("to come")*

In the dialogue, Jennifer says, **Il vient dans cette direction** ("It's coming in this direction"). **Vient** is a form of the irregular verb **venir** ("to come").

Here are the present tense forms of **venir**.

je **viens**	Je **viens** de Paris. *I come/I am from Paris.*
tu **viens**	**Viens**-tu au cinéma? *Are you coming to the movies?*
il/elle/on **vient**	On **vient** à midi. *We're coming at noon.*
nous **venons**	Nous ne **venons** pas ce soir. *We're not coming tonight.*
vous **venez**	Vous **venez** de l'aéroport. *You're coming from the airport.*
ils **viennent**	Ils **viennent** travailler. *They're coming to work.*

NOTE: **Revenir** ("to return") and **devenir** ("to become") are also conjugated like **venir**.

Le passé immédiat · *Immediate past*

Venir de expresses the idea of "coming from" or "having just accomplished something."

Je **viens de** Paris.	*I come from (I'm arriving from) Paris.*

Venir de can also be used to express an action that has just taken place. In such an instance, it is followed by a verb in the infinitive.

Voulez-vous un sandwich?	*Would you like a sandwich?*
Non, merci, **je viens de manger**.	*No thanks, I have just eaten.*
Nous venons de voir le Tour de France.	*We have just seen the Tour de France.*

◄ 9.6 ►
Audio exercise

Answer the questions on the recording, using the correct form of **venir** according to the model.

EXAMPLE

PROMPT   Voulez-vous boire?

RESPONSE   Non, je viens de boire.

◄ 9.7 ►
Exercise

Complete the following sentences with the correct form of **venir** or **venir de**.

1. Marie _____ arriver de Londres dans l'Eurostar.

2. Nos trois amis _____ New York et

    ils _____ visiter les grottes de Lascaux.

3. _____-tu dîner ce soir?

4. _____ par ici, s'il vous plaît.

5. Ces bons vins _____ Bourgogne.

6. Elle _____ souvent nous rendre visite.

7. On _____ apprécier un Kir royal au wagon-restaurant.

8. Ne _____ pas dans la matinée,

    _____ dans la soirée.

9. Je _____ faire trois kilomètres.

10. D'où _____-tu?

◄ **9.8** ►
DIALOGUE 2
Un pique-nique en Dordogne · *A picnic in Dordogne*

Our three friends go to the village to shop for food for their picnic.

Les trois «J» vont au village faire des courses pour préparer le pique-nique.

JEREMY	Moi, je viens de manger, je n'ai pas très faim, j'ai soif. Mais je peux manger un peu de pain.
JENNIFER	Bien, allons faire des courses, je vais à la boulangerie acheter le pain et toi, tu vas acheter les fromages.
JEREMY	Où est-ce que je vais les acheter?
JENNIFER	À la crémerie.
JEREMY	Qu'est-ce que je prends?
JENNIFER	J'aime le chèvre, alors pour moi un chèvre. Je l'aime bien fait.
M. JONES	Pour moi un Port-Salut. Et où est-ce que je dois aller?
JENNIFER	Allez à la charcuterie pour prendre quelques tranches de jambon et un peu de mortadelle. Ensuite, passez chez le marchand de vin. Surtout, n'oubliez pas d'acheter deux bouteilles d'eau minérale.
M. JONES	Alors, une plate et une pétillante, et pour les vins?
JEREMY	Un bon vin du pays.
JENNIFER	Faites vite car je meurs de faim.

Now listen again to the dialogue, and repeat after the speaker.

◄ **9.9** ►
Petit lexique

la boulangerie	*bakery*
la charcuterie	*(pork) butcher shop*
le chèvre	*goat cheese*
chez	*at the home of*
la crémerie	*dairy (store)*
faire des courses	*to go shopping*
faire vite	*to hurry*
le jambon	*ham*
le marchand de vin	*wine merchant*
la mortadelle	*mortadella (cold cut)*

mourir de faim	to starve
oublier	to forget
le pain	bread
le pique-nique	picnic
la tranche	slice
le vin du pays	local wine

Extension de vocabulaire

le supermarché	supermarket
la boucherie	butcher shop
l'épicerie (f.)	grocery (store)
le traiteur	gourmet deli
la pharmacie	pharmacy, drugstore
la librairie	bookstore
la laverie automatique	laundromat
l'électroménager (m.)	household appliance
la boutique/le magasin de souvenirs-cadeaux	gift store
la bijouterie	jewelry store
la boutique de vêtements	clothing store

◄ 9.10 ►
Compréhension et expressions

Expressions avec *faire*

In Chapter 4, you learned how to use the verb **faire**. In this dialogue, Jennifer says, **Allons faire les courses** ("Let's go shopping/Let's go run errands"). She also says, **Faites vite!** ("Hurry up!")

The verb **faire** is also used in other phrases.

faire la lessive	to do laundry
faire la vaisselle	to do the dishes
faire le ménage	to clean the house
faire la cuisine	to cook
faire le mort	to play dead

Je n'aime pas **faire la vaisselle**; heureusement nous avons un lave-vaisselle.   *I don't like doing dishes; fortunately, we have a dishwasher.*

> Ma grand-mère est un
>   cordon-bleu, elle adore
>   **faire la cuisine**.
>
> *My grandmother is a*
>   *cordon-bleu cook; she*
>   *loves to cook.*

Choisir un fromage ou une viande

When selecting cheese in France, it is useful to know the follow-ing expressions.

trop frais	*too fresh, not ripe enough (usually not very palatable)*
bien frais	*fresh (usually for soft cheeses)*
bien fait	*ripe*
trop fait	*too ripe (not pleasant to eat)*

When ordering meat in a restaurant, it is useful to know the fol-lowing expressions.

cru	*raw (like steak tartare)*
bleu	*very rare, close to raw*
saignant	*medium rare*
à point	*well done*
bien cuit	*extremely well done (tends to be overcooked)*

J'aime la viande **bien cuite**.   *I like meat extremely well done.*

◄ 9.11 ►
Audio exercise

You are in a restaurant; the speaker on the recording will prompt you on how to order meat and cheese. Then, repeat the correct response after the speaker.

EXAMPLE

PROMPT   I would like my steak well done, please!
RESPONSE   Je voudrais mon steak à point, s'il vous plaît.

◄ 9.12 ►
Structure grammaticale
chez/à · *to/at*

In the dialogue, our friends talk about going to different stores to shop for their picnic. In some instances, they say **chez**.

   chez le marchand de vin   *to/at the wine merchant's*

And in other instances, they use the preposition **à**.

à la crémerie	*to/at the cheese shop*
à la boulangerie	*to/at the bakery*
à la charcuterie	*to/at the butcher shop*
	(specializing in pork products)

Notice that when we speak of the store owner, we use **chez**.

chez le boulanger	*to/at the baker's*
chez le boucher	*to/at the butcher's*
chez l'épicier	*to/at the grocer's*

And when we speak of the store or place of business, we use **à**.

à la boulangerie	*to/at the bakery*
à la boucherie	*to/at the butcher shop*
à l'épicerie	*to/at the grocery*

You can say either **Je vais** *chez le boulanger* **pour acheter des croissants** ("to the baker's") or **Je vais** *à la boulangerie* **pour acheter des croissants** ("to the bakery").

◄ 9.13 ►
Exercise

Complete the following sentences with the correct preposition: **chez** or **à**.

1. Jeremy a trop mangé, il doit aller _____ le docteur.

2. Ensuite, il doit passer _____ la pharmacie pour acheter des médicaments.

3. On peut acheter des fromages _____ la crémerie et des tranches de jambon _____ le charcutier.

4. Les amis vont aller _____ le boulanger,

   _____ la pâtisserie, _____ le marchand de vin,

   _____ l'épicerie et _____ le traiteur pour préparer le pique-nique.

5. Notre chien Fido n'aime pas aller _____ le vétérinaire.

◄ 9.14 ►
Structure grammaticale

Les pronoms objets directs · *Direct object pronouns*

An object pronoun is a word that replaces a noun following the verb in a sentence. This noun is known as the direct object and answers the question "what" or "whom."

Il a mangé **le croissant**.	*He ate the croissant.*

What did he eat? **Le croissant** is the direct object.

Elle a vu **Pierre**.	*She saw Pierre.*

Whom did she see? **Pierre** is the direct object.

The forms **le/la/l'/les** are direct object pronouns.

In the exchange between Jeremy and Jennifer in the dialogue above, we encountered:

J'aime **le chèvre**... Je **l'**aime bien fait.	*I like goat cheese . . . I like it ripe.*
Tu vas acheter **les fromages**... Où est-ce que tu vas **les** acheter?	*You're going to buy the cheeses . . . Where are you going to buy them?*

In these two statements, **l'** and **les** are direct object pronouns. They replace, respectively, **le chèvre** and **les fromages**, which are direct objects.

le	*replaces a masculine direct object*
la	*replaces a feminine direct object*
l'	*masculine or feminine, is used when the verb starts with a vowel or silent* **h**
les	*replaces a plural direct object*

NOTE: Direct object pronouns are placed before the verb and cannot be separated from it.

Elle aime **le chocolat**.	Elle **l'**aime.
Elle n'aime pas **le chocolat**.	Elle ne **l'**aime pas.
Il regarde **son père**.	*He looks at his father.*
Il **le** regarde.	*He looks at him.*
Elle mange **la mousse au chocolat**. Elle **la** mange.	*She eats the chocolate mousse. She eats it.*

> Nous aimons **le champagne**. *We like champagne.*
>   Nous **l'**aimons.   *We like it.*
> Ils aiment **leurs amis**.   *They like their friends.*
>   Ils **les** aiment.   *They like them.*

 ◄ **9.15** ►
Audio exercise

Answer the questions on the recording in the affirmative, using the direct object pronoun. Then, repeat the correct answer after the speaker.

EXAMPLE

PROMPT   Regardez-vous la télé le soir?
RESPONSE   Oui, je la regarde.

 ◄ **9.16** ►
Audio exercise

Listen to the questions, and answer affirmatively in the past tense, using a direct object pronoun. Then, repeat the correct answer after the speaker.

EXAMPLE

PROMPT   Tu as mangé le sandwich?
RESPONSE   Oui, je l'ai mangé.

◄ **9.17** ►
Exercise

Complete the following sentences with the object pronoun: **le**, **la**, **l'**, or **les**.

1. Cette femme promène son chien, elle _____ promène tous les jours à six heures du matin. (promène, *walks*)

2. Elle fait la vaisselle, car son mari ne _____ fait jamais.

3. Nous aimons les spécialités mexicaines, nous _____ aimons beaucoup.

4. Aimez-vous la moutarde? Je _____ aime surtout sur la viande.

5. Avez-vous rendu le livre à la bibliothèque?

   —Oui, je _____ ai rendu.

6 Est-ce que les amis ont préparé le pique-nique?

   —Oui, ils _____ ont préparé.

7. Quand faites-vous la lessive?

   —Nous _____ faisons le samedi matin.

8. Finissez-vous les devoirs avant de regarder la télévision?

   —Oui, nous _____ finissons.

 ◄ **9.18** ►
DIALOGUE 3
En Bourgogne · *In Burgundy*

After a few days in Dordogne, our friends have arrived in Burgundy, where they are visiting the famous vineyards.

Après quelques jours en Dordogne, nos amis sont arrivés en Bourgogne où ils visitent les domaines des grands crus de la région.

JEREMY	*Qui c'est qui fait glou glou?*
	C'est la bouteille, c'est la bouteille,
	Qui c'est qui fait glou glou?
	C'est la bouteille de chez nous.
M. JONES	Vous êtes saoul, ma parole!
JENNIFER	Mais non, il n'est pas ivre, il est heureux d'être en Bourgogne.
M. JONES	Jeremy, vous avez visité combien de caves?
JEREMY	Dix, douze, treize, j'ai oublié.
JENNIFER	Je sais qu'avec moi, il est allé dans huit domaines et chaque fois que nous sommes arrivés il a goûté au vin.
M. JONES	Ah, je comprends maintenant, chaque fois que vous êtes passé dans un domaine vous avez goûté au vin et vous avez fini le verre!
JENNIFER	Oui, et nous avons acheté deux bouteilles.
M. JONES	Et où sont ces bouteilles?
JEREMY	Elles sont parties. Vive la Bourgogne, vive la France!

Listen again to the dialogue, and repeat after the speaker.

◄ 9.19 ►
Petit lexique

chaque	*each*
le cru	*first-rate vineyard*
le domaine	*estate*
goûter	*to taste*
ivre	*drunk*
la parole	*spoken word*
saoul(e)	*drunk*
savoir	*to know*
vive	*long live*

◄ 9.20 ►
Compréhension et expressions

chaque fois · *each time, every time*

In everyday vernacular, **chaque** is used to express "everything" or "everybody."

En France **chaque** personne doit avoir une carte d'identité.	*In France everybody must have an ID card.*
Je fais de la bicyclette **chaque** jour.	*I ride my bicycle every day.*

Ma parole! · *Indeed!, Really!, For real!*

Mr. Jones says, **Vous êtes saoul, ma parole!** ("You are really drunk!")

Vive la France! · *Long live France!*

◄ 9.21 ►
Structure grammaticale

Le passé composé avec *être* · *The past tense with* être

Study the following dialogue.

JENNIFER Vous **êtes allé** à la charcuterie?

M. JONES Oui, et j'ai acheté du jambon. Et vous, vous **êtes allée** à la boulangerie?

JENNIFER   Oui, je **suis allée** à la boulangerie, ensuite je **suis passée**
à la crémerie pour retrouver Jeremy et nous **sommes
allés** ensemble à la poste où nous avons acheté des
timbres.

Note the verbs conjugated with **être** in the above conversation.

Vous êtes allé à la charcuterie.	*You went to the butcher shop.*
Vous êtes allée à la boulangerie.	*You went to the bakery.*
Je suis passée à la crémerie.	*I went to the dairy (store).*
Nous sommes allés à la poste.	*We went to the post office.*

The following seventeen verbs, also known as "verbs of movement," are used with the auxiliary verb **être** to form the **passé composé**. Their past participles are given in parentheses.

aller (allé)	venir (venu)
arriver (arrivé)	partir (parti)
entrer (entré)	sortir (sorti)
monter (monté)	descendre (descendu)
naître ("to be born") (né)	mourir ("to die") (mort)
rester (resté)	tomber (tombé)
passer (passé)	devenir (devenu)
retourner (retourné)	revenir (revenu)
rentrer (rentré)	

You have probably noticed that when the verb is conjugated with **être**, the past participle agrees with the subject in gender and number.

Il est all**é** à la banque.	Elle est all**ée** au théâtre.
Ils sont all**és** à la banque.	Elles sont all**ées** au théâtre.

These sentences are made negative and interrogative in the same way as with the **avoir** verbs.

Je **ne suis pas entré** à la boulangerie.	*I didn't go into the bakery.*
Elle **n'est pas descendue** au rez-de-chaussée.	*She didn't come down to the first (ground) floor.*
À quelle heure **es-tu arrivé**?	*What time did you arrive?*
Sont-ils venus de Lyon?	*Did they come from Lyons?*

◄ 9.22 ►
Audio exercise

Listen to the questions on the recording, and answer in the affirmative. Then, repeat the correct answer after the speaker.

EXAMPLE

PROMPT   Tu es allé(e) à Dijon?

RESPONSE   Oui, je suis allé(e) à Dijon.

◄ 9.23 ►
Exercise

Complete the following sentences with the correct form of the verb in the **passé composé**.

1. Jennifer et Jeremy _____ du Louvre. (sortir)

2. Elle _____ au deuxième étage. (monter)

3. Ils _____ en Bourgogne. (aller)

4. Elles _____ dans le restaurant. (entrer)

5. Il _____ à Londres. (mourir)

6. L'avion _____ à Sydney. (arriver)

7. Elle _____ à la cave. (descendre)

8. Ils _____ à la bibliothèque. (retourner)

9. Il _____ français. (devenir)

10. Elle _____ à Montréal. (partir)

◄ 9.24 ►
Exercise

Complete the following sentences with the correct form of the verb in the **passé composé**. Choose carefully between **être** and **avoir.**

1. J'_____ la télé avec mes amis. (regarder)

2. Tu _____ ton devoir de français. (finir)

3. Nous _____ dans les grottes de Lascaux. (descendre)

4. Il _____ sa bicyclette. (vendre)

5. Ils ne _____ pas _____ en Afrique. (partir)

6. _____ elle _____ en retard? (arriver)

7. Ils n'_____ pas _____ leurs amis. (voir)

8. Elle _____ au Portugal. (aller)

9. _____-vous _____ à Dijon? (naître)

10. Marie-Claude _____ avec Pierre. (sortir)

11. Ils n'_____ pas _____ le métro. (prendre)

12. Nous _____ le dernier film de Gérard Depardieu. (voir)

 ◄ 9.25 ►
Audio practice

On the recording, listen to the reading of a poem by Jacques Prévert.

Déjeuner du matin

Il a mis le café
Dans la tasse
Il a mis le lait
Dans la tasse de café
Il a mis le sucre
Dans le café au lait
Avec la petite cuiller
Il a tourné
Il a bu le café au lait
Et il a reposé la tasse
Sans me parler
Il a allumé
Une cigarette
Il a fait des ronds

Avec la fumée
Il a mis les cendres
Dans le cendrier
Sans me parler
Sans me regarder
Il s'est levé
Il a mis
Son chapeau sur sa tête
Il a mis
Son manteau de pluie
Parce qu'il pleuvait
Et il est parti
Sous la pluie
Sans une parole
Sans me regarder
Et moi j'ai pris
Ma tête dans ma main
Et j'ai pleuré.

Listen to the poem again, and repeat after the speaker. This will help you remember past tense forms.

◄ **9.26** ►
Petit lexique

allumer	*to light*
la cendre	*ash*
la cigarette	*cigarette*
la fumée	*smoke*
se lever	*to stand up, to get up*
la main	*hand*
le manteau imperméable/ de pluie	*raincoat*
pleurer	*to cry*
le rond	*ring*
tourner	*to stir*

◄ **9.27** ►
Expressions

il pleuvait	*it was raining*
sans me parler	*without speaking to me*
sans me regarder	*without looking at me*

◄ 9.28 ►
Audio exercise

On the recording, answer the questions about the poem by Jacques Prévert. Then, repeat the correct answer after the speaker.

EXAMPLE

PROMPT   Qu'est-ce qu'il a mis dans la tasse?
RESPONSE   Il a mis le café.

◄ 9.29 ►
Common pitfalls

When using the past tense (**passé composé**), it is very easy to make mistakes, especially with the use of the auxiliary. Using **avoir** for **être** or vice versa is fairly common, and it can lead to amusing misunderstandings. Listen to the class interaction on the recording between the student and the teacher.

The misunderstanding here stems from the fact that the student has used **être** as an auxiliary, which puts the sentence into the passive voice, not the active. Therefore, when trying to say "I ate" (**j'*ai* mangé**), the student ends up saying "I am being eaten" (**je *suis* mangé**). When using the **passé composé**, it is important to use the correct auxiliary (**avoir** or **être**) to avoid such embarrassing situations.

◄ 9.30 ►
Let's take a plunge!

In this final chapter, you will test your aural comprehension skills by taking an even deeper plunge into French. On the recording, you will hear the speaker talking about France in the past tense (**passé composé**). Pay close attention, then answer out loud the questions that follow.

Here are some words you might need to understand the story. Study them first!

ainsi que	*as well as*
le chercheur/la chercheuse	*research scientist*
lacustre	*lakeside (village or home)*
longtemps	*for a long time*
en particulier	*particularly*

◄ 9.31 ►
Vive la différence!

Design of French villages and towns

It is only in the more modern villages and towns of France, those rebuilt after the destruction of World Wars I and II, that a geometric design of parallel and perpendicular intersecting streets has been established. In most traditional communities, the streets radiate from a central point in the town like the spokes of a wheel or the rays of a star (the Place Charles de Gaulle in Paris is a typical example). For centuries, the church formed the center of French communities, but after the Revolution, the **mairie** ("town hall") became the center of village and town life.

La Bourgogne · *Burgundy*

Bourgogne, the fabled region of France, was an independent kingdom during the Middle Ages. It is renowned for its medieval towns, black slate roofs, and, like all French provinces, its culinary specialties. **La moutarde de Dijon, les escargots de Bourgogne**, and **le vol-au-vent**, a delicious flaky-crust meat pie, are just a few examples. From **Bourgogne** also come some of the world's most exalted wines, including two of France's most popular: **Chablis** and **Beaujolais**.

Winemaking was already a well-established art when the Romans conquered the region in the first century B.C. In the sixth century, one of the kings of Burgundy initiated a far-reaching custom: he gave his vineyards to the Church. This practice would continue until the French Revolution, when the vineyards owned by monasteries were confiscated and sold to the people.

◄ **9.32** ►
Activities

To mark the completion of chapters 7 through 9, and of the
En français course, try these activities.

A. Choisir un bon vin! Pouvez-vous lire l'étiquette sur une
bouteille de vin?

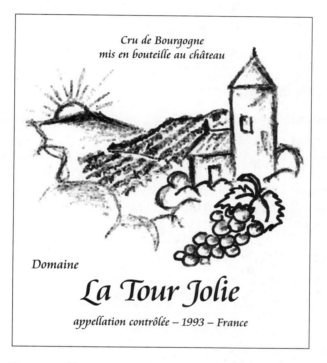

*Cru de Bourgogne
mis en bouteille au château*

Domaine

La Tour Jolie

appellation contrôlée – 1993 – France

1. Dans quelle région de France ce vin a-t-il été fait?

   _____

2. Où est-ce que le vin a été mis en bouteille? (mis en
   bouteille, *bottled*) _____

3. C'est un cru de quelle année? _____

4. Comment pouvez-vous savoir que c'est un vin d'origine?

   _____

B. **Calembours** ("Puns"). Here are some puns based on sound similarities. Can you create some yourself?

OBIC   obéissez
M qui TM   aime qui t'aime

Now, try to answer the following questions by saying the following phrases out loud.

1. **Il est tout vert.**

   What did the happy thief say about the safe?

   _____

2. **La bouche rit.**

   Where do you buy meat? _____

3. **C'est un neuf.**

   What did the hen say to the rooster?

   _____

4. **Le premier homme du monde.**

   It's also the world's first what?

   _____

5. **Un effort.**

   What did Cyrano de Bergerac suffer from?

   _____

Answer key

1 Bonjour · *Hello*

1.14 1. Il 2. Nous 3. Ils OR Elles 4. Je 5. Vous 6. Tu 7. Elles
8. Tu 9. Elle

1.15 1. est 2. sont 3. suis 4. es 5. sont 6. sommes 7. êtes
8. est 9. est 10. est

1.18 1. plumber 2. dentist 3. receptionist 4. electrician
5. mechanic 6. technician 7. veterinarian 8. secretary 9. doctor
10. professor/teacher

1.20

(Je vais) bien OR pas mal OR comme-ci comme-ça, merci.

Je suis OR Je m'appelle (give your name).

Je suis Américain(e) OR Anglais(e) (give your nationality; if necessary,
look it up in a dictionary).

Je suis docteur OR professeur (give your profession; if necessary, look it up
in a dictionary).

Je suis de (give the name of your town).

Au revoir!

2 Plans de voyage · *Travel plans*

2.8 1. travaillons 2. habitent 3. jouez 4. aimes 5. regardons
6. parle

2.9 1. parlons 2. travaille 3. aime 4. adorez 5. jouez 6. réserve
7. regarde 8. habitent 9. écoutent 10. commences

2.14 1. Les, la 2. la 3. Les, les 4. L' 5. Les 6. Le, le, les, le
7. le, la 8. La

2.15 1. aime, la 2. Les, utilisent, les 3. Le, les, parlent 4. adorent, la
5. La, le, sont, les

2.22 1. Nous aimons marcher sur le sable. 2. Il fait du vent à
Strasbourg. 3. Elle aime nager dans la mer (en mer). 4. En hiver,
Catherine et André aiment faire du ski (skier). 5. Le matin, il pleut
à Brest. 6. Martine travaille la nuit. 7. M. et Mme Dupont aiment
voyager en été. 8. En hiver, il neige à Lyon.

2.23

PROFESSEUR   La télévision marche bien.

ÉTUDIANT   Je marche? Elle marche? la personne marche; la télévision, elle marche?

PROFESSEUR   Oui, la télévision marche bien! Elle fonctionne bien, elle marche bien. Une personne marche: circule. La télévision marche: fonctionne.

2.24

Oui, ça marche bien.

Oui, je parle un peu français.

J'habite à (name the city where you live).

Je travaille à (name the place where you work).

Moi aussi. OR J'aime les films d'action. OR J'aime les comédies.

Moi aussi. OR Oui, j'aime jouer au tennis. (le tennis, non!)

En hiver, il fait (très) froid OR il neige.

Au revoir!

3   Parlons vacances! · *Let's talk about vacation!*

3.11   1. a, a   2. ont   3. avons   4. a   5. avez   6. ai, as, avons   7. a
8. a

3.15   1. Non, je ne parle pas anglais.   2. Non, elle ne travaille pas à l'aéroport.   3. Non, ils n'ont pas soif.   4. Non, nous n'avons pas faim.
5. Non, on n'aime pas le football.   6. Non, je n'ai pas sommeil.

3.22   1. anglaise   2. japonais   3. canadienne   4. français   5. italien
6. chinois   7. américains   8. espagnol   9. cubain   10. mexicaine

3.27   1. grand   2. vert   3. blonds   4. amoureuse   5. chaleureuse
6. fatiguée, irritable   7. sincères, timides   8. impulsive

3.28

PROFESSEUR   Vous désirez manger, qu'est-ce que vous dites?

ÉTUDIANT   Je suis faim!

PROFESSEUR   Non, vous n'êtes pas faim, vous êtes Peter!

ÉTUDIANT   Oui, je suis Peter, je suis américain et je suis faim!

PROFESSEUR   Non, vous êtes Peter, vous êtes américain et vous avez faim.

3.29

Oui, j'ai faim. OR Non, je n'ai pas faim.

Moi aussi. OR Je suis fatigué. (Je ne suis pas fatigué.) BUT J'ai soif. (Je n'ai pas soif.)

Oui, je suis optimiste. OR Non, je ne suis pas optimiste.

Oui, je suis irritable. OR Non, je ne suis pas irritable.

J'aime le coca-cola OR (Et) la bière OR (Et) le jus d'orange.

(Moi aussi) au revoir.

3.32

A 1. Salut! 2. Bonjour! 3. Au revoir. 4. Merci. 5. Bonne nuit.
6. Bonjour, Mademoiselle. 7. Bonjour, Messieurs-dames. 8. Allô!

B 1. Joyeux anniversaire! 2. Je suis en retard. 3. Bonne chance!
4. Au secours! 5. Excusez-moi/Désolé(e).

C 1. Astérix 2. Niagara Falls (les chutes du Niagara) 3. Napoleon
Bonaparte 4. the Statue of Liberty (la statue de la Liberté) 5. Mona Lisa
(La Joconde)

4 Les trois « J » à Paris · *The three "J"s in Paris*

4.7 1. voudrais, s'il vous plaît 2. voudrais, s'il vous plaît 3. voudrais,
s'il te plaît 4. voudrais, s'il vous plaît 5. voudrais, s'il te plaît

4.8 1. aux 2. au 3. à la 4. aux 5. au 6. à la 7. au 8. à la
9. à la 10. à l'

4.11 1. Paul et Patrick, ne jouez pas au basket! 2. Visitons la France.
3. Étienne, travaille à Paris! 4. Montons à la tour Eiffel. 5. Écoutez
le professeur! 6. Parlons français! 7. Anne, mange le gâteau!
8. Regardons le numéro de téléphone. 9. Françoise, Karine et Sabrine,
visitez le musée du Louvre! 10. Laurent, compte!

4.17 1. Un 2. un, une 3. des, un 4. une, un 5. une 6. une

4.18 1. la 2. un 3. un 4. une 5. le

4.19

Qu'est-ce que vous **prenez** Messieurs-dames?

Les amis commandent **des** boissons. Jennifer **prend un** lait-fraise,
Jeremy et M. Jones **prennent une** bouteille d'eau minérale. Le garçon arrive
avec **une** bouteille de champagne. M. Jones explique qu'ils ne désirent pas
une bouteille de champagne, mais **une** bouteille d'eau minérale. Le garçon
est furieux et il ne **comprend** pas. Il répète: **apprenez** le français!

4.22 1. Moi 2. Elle 3. Eux 4. Nous 5. moi 6. Vous 7. Toi
8. Nous, eux

4.26 1. 48 2. 29 3. 50 4. 37 5. 19 6. 56

4.30 1. Il est vingt heures trente. 2. Il est douze heures dix. 3. Il est
quinze heures dix. 4. Il est vingt et une heures dix. 5. Il est seize heures
quarante. 6. Il est vingt et une heures quarante.

4.33 Quel temps **fait**-il à Boston? Le matin, à Nice, il **fait du** soleil. Je **fais de la** natation et Antoine **fait du** tennis. L'après-midi, il pleut souvent mais ça ne **fait** rien; nous **faisons la** sieste. Le soir, j'aime **faire du** shopping. Quelquefois on **fait un** tour. Ne t'en **fais** pas pour moi. Je suis en pleine forme. **Fais un** bisou aux amis.

4.34

PROFESSEUR	Et après la salade et le fromage?
ÉTUDIANT	Je voudrais le *désert*, s'il vous plaît!
PROFESSEUR	Ah, je suis désolé, Monsieur, mais en France il n'y a pas le *désert*, pour cela, il faut aller en Afrique du Nord ou en Arizona.
ÉTUDIANT	Pourquoi l'Afrique du Nord, l'Arizona, il n'y a pas de *désert* à Paris?
PROFESSEUR	Ah, non, monsieur, désolé.
ÉTUDIANT	Comment, vous n'avez pas de fruits, de glace à la vanille, etc...?
PROFESSEUR	Oh, mais bien sûr, vous voulez dire *dessert*, pas *désert*.

4.35

Je voudrais un café, s'il vous plaît.

Un café au lait.

Non merci. Quelle heure est-il?

Je voudrais aller au musée d'Orsay.

C'est combien? OR Ça fait combien?

Voilà trois euros cinquante.

5 À l'hôtel · *At the hotel*

5.6 1. Avez-vous une chambre climatisée? 2. Avez-vous une chambre double? 3. Avez-vous un sauna? 4. Jennifer a-t-elle une réservation? 5. Jouons-nous au basket? 6. Jennifer et M. Jones désirent-ils un Perrier-citron? 7. Aimons-nous la tour Eiffel? 8. Le président français habite-t-il à l'Élysée? 9. Avons-nous des amis? 10. Avons-nous une salle de bains?

5.10 1. 22–33, vingt-deux–trente-trois 2. 41–51, quarante et un–cinquante et un 3. 19–28, dix-neuf–vingt-huit 4. 66–86, soixante-six–quatre-vingt-six 5. 81–92, quatre-vingt-un–quatre-vingt-douze 6. 77–16, soixante-dix-sept–seize 7. 10–112, dix–cent douze 8. 36–671, trente-six–six cent soixante et onze

5.11 1. C'est le vingt et un juillet. 2. C'est le quinze août. 3. C'est le huit mai. 4. C'est le vingt-cinq décembre. 5. C'est le premier mai. 6. C'est le premier août. 7. C'est le quatre juillet. 8. C'est le premier novembre.

5.17 1. veut 2. pouvez 3. veut 4. doivent 5. peux 6. doivent
7. dois 8. doit 9. peuvent 10. voulons

5.18 1. doivent OR veulent 2. doit 3. veut 4. peut, peut 5. Voulez
6. doivent 7. peut OR doit 8. veulent 9. doit 10. veulent

5.21

ÉTUDIANT	Pardon Madame, je *dois au* docteur.
PROFESSEUR	Qu'est-ce que vous *devez au* docteur?
ÉTUDIANT	Pardon, est-ce que je peux aller? Je *dois au* docteur.
PROFESSEUR	Qu'est-ce que vous *devez au* docteur? Combien d'argent?
ÉTUDIANT	Non, je suis malade aujourd'hui, je *dois au* docteur à deux heures.
PROFESSEUR	Ah, vous *devez aller* chez le docteur à deux heures. Je *dois aller.*

5.22

Elle veut téléphoner.

Elle veut téléphoner à Cannes.

Oui, elle a le numéro.

C'est le 04 (zéro-quatre).

C'est deux euros quatre-vingt-douze.

Elle peut acheter une télécarte.

Elle doit aller au bureau de tabac ou au bar.

6 Au Procope · *At the Procope*

6.7 1. à 2. de 3. à côté de 4. sur 5. sous 6. devant 7. derrière
8. sous 9. au milieu de 10. loin de

6.16 Au quartier Latin il y a **des** restaurants et **des** cafés-terrasse. Vous pouvez, si vous voulez, commander **des** spécialités françaises, **du** café, **du** thé ou **des** boissons. Si vous êtes gourmand, vous pouvez manger **de la** glace à la framboise, **des** crêpes, **de la** pêche Melba, **du** jus de pamplemousse, mais vous ne pouvez pas avoir **de** spécialités mexicaines ou brésiliennes dans un café français traditionnel.

6.23 Alice **est** une petite fille qui n'**obéit** pas. Elle **décide** de visiter le pays des Merveilles. Elle **rencontre** deux lapins qui **bâtissent** une maison en sucre dans un jardin magique. Dans le jardin, il y a aussi des fleurs en chocolat. Les lapins **invitent** Alice à entrer. Elle **prend** un grand panier. Alice et les deux lapins **choisissent** les chocolats et ils **remplissent** le panier.

6.26 Le week-end, je **sors** avec Isabelle. Nous **partons** à huit heures du matin pour aller à la campagne. Nous **partons** en train jusqu'à Chartres. En général, Isabelle **dort** dans le train, car elle aime dormir. Quand nous arrivons à Chartres, nous **sortons** de la gare pour aller déjeuner dans un petit café. Isabelle veut commander une pizza; le garçon dit —Je suis désolé, nous ne **servons** pas de pizza, mais on **sert** des croque-monsieur.

6.27

ÉTUDIANTE   Je voudrais un verre *de* vin, s'il vous plaît.

PROFESSEUR   Vous avez déjà un verre de vin rouge, vous désirez un autre verre?

ÉTUDIANTE   Oui, Monsieur.

PROFESSEUR   Rouge ou blanc?

ÉTUDIANTE   Ce n'est pas important, c'est comme vous voulez.

PROFESSEUR   Si, c'est important, c'est vous qui allez le boire. Alors rouge ou blanc?

ÉTUDIANTE   C'est pour donner un peu de vin à mon ami.

PROFESSEUR   Ah, ce n'est pas un verre *de* vin que vous voulez, mais un verre *à* vin.

6.28

La France est un grand pays européen. C'est un pays moderne avec une importante technologie et une riche tradition historique et culturelle.

    Il y a en France beaucoup de monuments et de musées intéressants. Les différentes régions de France présentent toutes une identité particulière avec des spécialités gastronomiques de renommée mondiale.

    Par exemple, les vins de Bourgogne et les fromages de Normandie sont célèbres dans le monde entier. La réputation et l'élégance de certaines villes comme Paris n'est plus à faire.

1. C'est un grand pays européen.
2. Elle a une tradition historique et une tradition culturelle.
3. Il y a beaucoup de monuments et de musées intéressants.
4. Les vins pour la Bourgogne et les fromages pour la Normandie. OR En Bourgogne les vins sont célèbres et en Normandie les fromages.
5. La réputation et l'élégance de Paris n'est plus à faire.

6.31

A   1. Montélimar   2. Dijon   3. Strasbourg   4. Normandie   5. Cognac 6. Cambrai   7. Toulouse   8. Bourgogne

B   1. une doctoresse   2. une nièce   3. une sœur   4. une Algérienne 5. une belle-fille   6. une présidente   7. une Française   8. rapide 9. mesdames   10. fille

7   La visite de Paris · *Touring Paris*

7.6   1. attendons   2. perd   3. vendez   4. rend   5. répond 6. prétendent

7.7   1. prétend   2. répondez   3. Entendez   4. attendent   5. vend
6. perdons

7.13   1. Oui, mon père parle français.   2. Oui, ma mère parle anglais.
3. Oui, son père est américain.   4. Oui, sa mère est américaine.   5. Oui,
Marie-France est sa petite amie.   6. Oui, c'est son stylo.

7.19   1. Son, ses   2. leurs   3. leur   4. ma   5. ta   6. votre   7. notre
8. votre

7.22   1. boivent   2. voit   3. voir   4. boit   5. boire   6. buvons
7. voit   8. voient

7.23

PROFESSEUR	Tiens, bonjour Roger, que faites-vous ici?
ÉTUDIANT	J'*entends* le train pour aller à New Haven, pour visiter mon ami qui *attend* l'université de Yale.
PROFESSEUR	Ah! Vous voulez dire que vous *attendez* le train, pour rendre visite à votre ami qui *va à* l'université de Yale à New Haven. Moi aussi, je *vais à* New Haven.
ÉTUDIANT	Non, je *vais à* Yale, mon ami *est à* Yale. Il *va à* l'université.
PROFESSEUR	Non, vous voulez vraiment dire, que vous *attendez* le train pour aller à New Haven pour rendre visite à votre ami qui *va à* Yale. Ah, mais j'*entends* notre train qui arrive!

7.24

Un touriste et son guide se promènent dans Paris. Quand ils passent devant
la cathédrale Notre-Dame, le touriste demande au guide:
  —Combien de temps a-t-il fallu pour construire la cathédrale?
  —Cent ans, répond le guide.
  —Cent ans, dit le touriste, dans mon pays, trente ans.
  Un peu plus tard, les deux amis passent devant le musée du Louvre.
Le touriste demande encore:
  —Et le Louvre, combien de temps pour le construire?
  —Cinquante ans, dit le guide.
  —Cinquante ans, répond le touriste avec ironie, dans mon pays,
cinq ans.
  Le guide est impatient, mais il ne dit rien. Quand ils arrivent devant
la tour Eiffel, le touriste demande:
  —Et la tour Eiffel, combien de temps pour la construire?
  —C'est bizarre, répond le guide, elle n'était pas ici hier.

1. Il est à Paris.
2. Le guide est avec le touriste.
3. Cent ans.   OR   Il a fallu cent ans.
4. Il est impatient.
5. Non, elle n'était pas ici hier.

8 Randonnée à travers la France · *Roaming across France*

8.4   1. Ils veulent visiter les grottes de Lascaux.   2. Les amis veulent visiter la « préhistoire ».   3. Elles sont en Dordogne.   4. On doit passer par Bordeaux.   5. On doit louer une voiture.   6. On peut prendre l'avion ou le TGV.   7. C'est le train à grande vitesse.

8.7   1. ce   2. Cette   3. ces   4. cet   5. ces, cet

8.14   1. Il a acheté du fromage.   2. Il a travaillé à la banque.
3. Ils ont chanté à l'Opéra.   4. Elle a choisi une bouteille de vin.
5. Il a répondu au téléphone.   6. Il a pris le train.

8.15   1. ai regardé   2. as fini   3. avez appris   4. a vendu   5. ont parlé
6. a choisi   7. ont attendu   8. ont mis   9. a fait   10. a bu

8.22   1. a vendu OR pris, choisi, acheté, visité, loué   2. Avez(-vous) loué, avez visité   3. (n')avons (pas) écouté   4. ai fait   5. avons attendu
6. a choisi   7. ont acheté OR vendu, pris, choisi   8. A(-t-elle) téléphoné

8.23

ÉTUDIANT   Monsieur, hier j'ai rendu visite à mon amie, elle habite à côté de la tour Eiffel, mais j'ai eu des problèmes.

PROFESSEUR   Pourquoi avez-vous eu des problèmes, John?

ÉTUDIANT   Parce que mon amie m'a donné une mauvaise adresse. Elle m'a dit que son appartement est au troisième étage, mais quand j'ai sonné à la porte de l'appartement au troisième étage, une dame a ouvert la porte et a dit, « Monsieur, ici, c'est le deuxième étage! » Je n'ai pas compris.

8.24

Un petit chat arrive à la maison. Il rentre de l'école; il est heureux et il aboie quand il voit la maman-chat. Sa mère est très surprise et elle lui demande pourquoi est-ce qu'il aboie.

—Tu es un petit chat, les petits chats n'aboient pas, ils miaulent, ce sont les petits chiens qui aboient.

Le petit chat répond:

—Je sais maman, mais aujourd'hui j'ai beaucoup étudié, j'ai appris une langue étrangère à l'école!

1. Il arrive à la maison.
2. Il aboie.
3. Les petits chats n'aboient pas. OR Les petits chats miaulent.
4. Ils aboient.
5. Il a appris une langue étrangère.

9 Provinces de France · *French provinces*

9.7   1. vient d'   2. viennent de, viennent de   3. Viens   4. Venez
5. viennent de   6. vient   7. vient d'   8. venez, venez   9. viens de
10. viens

9.13   1. chez   2. à   3. à, chez   4. chez, à, chez, à, chez   5. chez

9.17   1. le   2. la   3. les   4. l'   5. l'   6. l'   7. la   8. les

9.23   1. sont sortis   2. est montée   3. sont allés   4. sont entrées
5. est mort   6. est arrivé   7. est descendue   8. sont retournés   9. est
devenu   10. est partie

9.24   1. ai regardé   2. as fini   3. sommes descendus   4. a vendu
5. sont (pas) partis   6. Est(-elle) arrivée   7. ont (pas) vu   8. est allée
9. Êtes(-vous) né(e)(s)   10. est sortie   11. ont (pas) pris   12. avons vu

9.29

PROFESSEUR	Voulez-vous aller déjeuner avec moi?
ÉTUDIANT	Non merci, je *suis mangé*!
PROFESSEUR	Mais c'est terrible, qui vous mange?
ÉTUDIANT	Personne, je *suis mangé* seul avant la classe.
PROFESSEUR	Ah! Vous voulez dire que vous *avez mangé* avant la classe! Vous *avez mangé*.

9.30

Pendant longtemps la France a été une province romaine. Quand les
Romains sont arrivés en France, ils ont développé un important système
de communications et de très belles villes, comme Arles, Nîmes, Avignon
et Paris. Ce sont les Romains qui ont donné le nom de « Paris » au petit
village lacustre de Lutèce.

Depuis, la France, et Paris en particulier, sont devenus un centre de
culture internationale. Les grands philosophes comme Voltaire et Rousseau,
les grands chercheurs comme Louis Pasteur et Marie Curie, ainsi que les
grands couturiers, comme Dior ou Saint-Laurent ont tous contribué à
la réputation de la France.

1. Ils ont développé un important système de communications et de très
   belles villes.
2. Ils ont donné le nom de Paris au petit village de Lutèce.
3. Les villes d'Arles, Nîmes et Avignon ont été fondées par les Romains.
4. Ce sont de grands philosophes.
5. Ils ont contribué à la grandeur de la France.

9.32

A   1. en Bourgogne   2. au château   3. 1993   4. parce que c'est une
appellation contrôlée

B   1. Il est ouvert.   2. la boucherie   3. C'est un œuf.   4. le premier
rhum du monde   5. un nez fort

Grammar summary

La phrase simple · *The simple sentence*

subject	+ verb	+ object
(noun/pronoun)	(describes action)	(person/thing receiving action)
Pierre	**parle**	**français**

Les pronoms sujets · *Subject pronouns*

je	*I*
tu	*you (familiar/singular)*
il	*he*
elle	*she*
on	*one/we/they (impersonal form)*
nous	*we*
vous	*you*
ils/elles	*they*

Le verbe et le temps présent · *The verb and the present tense*

A verb is a word that describes the action in a sentence. French verbs are grouped into three basic conjugations according to their infinitive endings.

-er	-ir	-re
parl**er**	fin**ir**	vend**re**
("to speak")	("to finish")	("to sell")

Les verbes réguliers · *Regular verbs*

To conjugate a verb, we drop the infinitive ending (**-er/-ir/-re**) and add the endings for person and number.

je	parl-**e**	fin-**is**	vend-**s**
tu	parl-**es**	fin-**is**	vend-**s**
il/elle/on	parl-**e**	fin-**it**	vend-__
nous	parl-**ons**	fin-**issons**	vend-**ons**
vous	parl-**ez**	fin-**issez**	vend-**ez**
ils/elles	parl-**ent**	fin-**issent**	vend-**ent**

$$
\text{Le professeur} \begin{cases} \text{parle français.} \\ \text{finit la leçon.} \\ \text{vend des cassettes de français.} \end{cases}
$$

Les verbes irréguliers · *Irregular verbs*

Not all French verbs are regular. Each conjugation has some irregular, exception verbs.

-er	**-ir**	**-re**
appeler ("to call")	**sortir** ("to go out"), **partir, dormir, servir**	**prendre** ("to take"), **apprendre, comprendre**
j'appelle	je sors	je prends
tu appelles	tu sors	tu prends
il/elle/on appelle	il/elle/on sort	il/elle/on prend
nous appelons	nous sortons	nous prenons
vous appelez	vous sortez	vous prenez
ils/elles appellent	ils/elles sortent	ils/elles prennent

Notice that, for verbs like **appeler**, the irregularity is apparent in the stem of the verb in the first-, second-, and third-person singular and in the third-person plural. The **nous** and **vous** forms retain the original spelling of the infinitive.

acheter ("to buy")

j'achète
tu achètes
il/elle/on achète
nous achetons
vous achetez
ils/elles achètent

Notice the **accent grave** that appears in the first-, second-, and third-person singular and in the third-person plural. The **nous** and **vous** forms retain the original spelling of the infinitive.

boire ("to drink")

je bois
tu bois
il/elle/on boit
nous buvons
vous buvez
ils/elles boivent

Quatre verbes irréguliers usuels · *Four common irregular verbs*

être	avoir	aller	faire
("to be")	("to have")	("to go")	("to do," "to make")
je suis	j'ai	je vais	je fais
tu es	tu as	tu vas	tu fais
il/elle/on est	il/elle/on a	il/elle/on va	il/elle/on fait
nous sommes	nous avons	nous allons	nous faisons
vous êtes	vous avez	vous allez	vous faites
ils/elles sont	ils/elles ont	ils/elles vont	ils/elles font

NOTE: **Avoir** is followed by a noun, which is introduced by an article.

J'ai des amis.	*I have some friends.*
Elle a un livre de français.	*She has a French book.*

Être is followed by an adjective or a description of a state of mind or being.

Je suis américain.	*I am American.*
Elle est intelligente.	*She is intelligent.*
Nous sommes malades.	*We are sick.*

NOTE: The word following **être** agrees in gender and number with the subject of the sentence (in the examples above, **je**, **elle**, and **nous**).

The verb **aller** ("to go") is always followed by a preposition (the equivalent of "to," "into").

à la	*if the following word is feminine singular*
au	*if the following word is masculine singular*
à l'	*if the following word starts with a vowel or silent **h** (masculine or feminine)*
aux	*if the following word is plural*

NOTE: **Au** is a contraction of the preposition **à** and the article **le**.
Aux is a contraction of the preposition **à** and the article **les**.
À le and **à les** do not exist, so never try to use them.

Le futur proche avec *aller* · *The immediate future with* aller

Aller is used to form the immediate future tense.

aller	+ action verb in the infinitive	
Je vais	manger.	*I am going to eat.*
Nous allons	travailler.	*We are going to work.*
Elle va	étudier.	*She is going to study.*

Les articles · *Articles*

There are three groups of articles in French.

Definite article: le, la, les, l' ("the")

le   *before a masculine noun*
la   *before a feminine noun*
l'   *before a noun starting with a vowel or silent* **h** *(masculine or feminine)*
les   *before both masculine and feminine plural nouns*

Indefinite article: un, une, des ("a/an/some")

un   *before a masculine noun*
une   *before a feminine noun*
des   *before both masculine and feminine plural nouns*

Partitive: du, de la, de l', des ("some," "part of")

du   *before a masculine noun*
de la   *before a feminine noun*
de l'   *before a noun starting with a vowel or silent* **h** *(masculine or feminine)*
des   *before both masculine and feminine plural nouns*

NOTE: **Du** is a contraction of **de le.**
Des is a contraction of **de les.**
De le and **de les** do not exist and are never correct, so never try to use them.

La négation · *The negative form*

To negate an action, use the following formula.

subject + **ne/n'** + verb + **pas** + object

The verb is bracketed by the negation words.

ne/n' + verb + **pas**

NOTE: The contraction **n'** replaces **ne** if the verb that follows starts with a vowel or silent **h**.

On parle français.   *We speak French.*
On **ne** parle **pas** espagnol.   *We don't speak Spanish.*
Il **n'**aime **pas** les chocolats.   *He doesn't like chocolates.*

Négation de l'article indéfini et du partitif ·
Negation of the indefinite article and the partitive

Un/une/du/de la/de l'/des become **pas de** or **pas d'** in a negative sentence.

Je mange du chocolat.	*I eat chocolate.*
Je **ne** mange **pas de** chocolat.	*I don't eat chocolate.*

NOTE: This rule applies only to the indefinite article and the partitive; it does not affect the definite articles **le, la, l', les**.

J'aime le chocolat.	*I like chocolate.*
Je **n'**aime **pas** le chocolat.	*I don't like chocolate.*

Les questions · *Questions*

There are three ways to formulate a question in French.

- Raising the tone of voice at the end of a sentence

Il est Français?	*Is he French?*

- Placing the expression **est-ce que/qu'** at the beginning of the sentence or in front of a positive statement

  Il est français.
  Est-ce qu'il est français?

- Inverting the order of the verb and the subject pronoun

  subject (pronoun) + verb + object
  verb + subject pronoun + object

  If the subject is a noun, it must be replaced by the equivalent pronoun.

  Pierre est français.
  Est-il français?

  The pronoun **il** replaces **Pierre** to allow the inversion.

  The subject noun (**Pierre**) may also be retained.

  Pierre est français.
  Pierre est-il français?

  A **-t-** is inserted between the verb and the subject pronoun to prevent the jarring sound of two vowels together.

  Il parle français.
  Parle-**t**-il français?

  When this is not the case, **-t-** is not used.

  Nous parlons français.
  Parlons-nous français?

Mots qui servent à former des questions · *Question words*

Placed at the beginning of a question, these words add a new meaning and dimension (condition/manner, place, reason, time, or subject of action) to a question.

Condition, manner

Comment?	*How?*
Comment allez-vous?	*How are you?* (Here it applies to the well-being of a person.)
Comment allez-vous en France, en train ou en avion?	*How are you going to France, by train or by plane?*

Place

Où?	*Where?*
Où allez-vous?	*Where are you going?*
Nous allons au cinéma.	*We are going to the movies.*

Reason

Pourquoi?	*Why?*
Pourquoi allez-vous au cinéma?	*Why are you going to the movies?*

The answer to such a question usually starts with **parce que/qu'** ("because").

Parce que nous aimons les films.	*Because we like films.*

NOTE: Sometimes the answer to **pourquoi?** can be introduced by the preposition **pour** ("in order to") followed by a verb of action in the infinitive.

Nous allons au cinéma pour voir un film.	*We are going to the movies (in order) to see a film.*

Time

Quand?	*When?*
Quand allez-vous au cinéma? Quand est-ce que vous allez au cinéma?	*When are you going to the movies?*

Subject of action

Qui?	*Who?*
Avec qui?	*With whom?*
Avec qui allez-vous au cinéma? Avec qui est-ce que vous allez au cinéma?	*With whom are you going to the movies?*

Réponses aux questions · *Answering questions*

Oui ("yes") is used when the answer is in agreement with a positive question or a statement by the other person.

Vous parlez français?	*Do you speak French?*
Oui, nous parlons français.	*Yes, we speak French.*

Si ("yes," "of course") is used to express a positive answer to a negative question or statement (to express that your point of view is positively contrary to what is being asked or stated).

Vous ne parlez pas français?	*Don't you speak French?*

If you actually speak French and you want to answer that you do speak French, you answer:

Si, je parle français.	*Of course, I speak French.*

NOTE: **Non** answers any question or statement you disagree with.

Parlez-vous espagnol?	*Do you speak Spanish?*
Non, nous ne parlons pas espagnol, nous parlons français.	*No, we don't speak Spanish; we speak French.*

Les adjectifs démonstratifs · *Demonstrative adjectives*

ce ⎫ cet ⎭	masculine singular	*this/that*
cette	feminine singular	*this/that*
ces	feminine and masculine plural	*these/those*

Demonstrative adjectives are used to identify a person, an object, or a thing.

Note the **cet** form for the masculine; it is used when the following word begins with a vowel or silent **h**.

ce garçon	*this boy*
cet homme	*this man*
cette femme	*this woman*
ces garçons	*these boys*
ces hommes	*these men*
ces femmes	*these women*

Le passé composé · *The past tense*

Composé means "composed or compounded of more than one word." This is the most common past tense in the French language. It is formed with the auxiliary verb (**avoir** or **être**) in the present tense + the past participle of the verb describing the action.

Avoir is used as the auxiliary verb with most French verbs; they are called "verbs of action."

Être is used with a set of specific verbs called "verbs of movement" or "verbs of motion." These verbs can be grouped in opposite pairs according to their meaning.

aller	entrer	arriver	monter	rester	naître
venir	sortir	partir	descendre	tomber	mourir

Other verbs of this type are **passer, retourner, devenir,** and all the reflexive verbs.

Le passé composé avec *avoir* · *Passé composé with* avoir

This tense is formed by conjugating **avoir** in the present tense and following it with the past participle of a verb of action.

j'**ai**	**parlé**
tu **as**	**parlé**
il/elle/on **a**	**parlé**
nous **avons**	**parlé**
vous **avez**	**parlé**
ils/elles **ont**	**parlé**

J'ai parlé français à Paris.	*I spoke/I have spoken French in Paris.*
Nous avons parlé français à Paris.	*We spoke/We have spoken French in Paris.*

Notice that the past participle used with **avoir** does not change in any of the conjugation forms: **je, tu, il, elle, on, nous, vous, ils, elles.**

EXCEPTION: The past participle agrees in gender and number if the direct object (usually in the form of a direct object pronoun) is placed before it.

Ta lettre? Je l'ai mise sur le bureau.	*Your letter? I put it on the desk.*

Le passé composé avec *être* · *Passé composé with* être

This tense is formed by conjugating **être** in the present tense and following it with the past participle.

je suis arrivé (*m.*)/arrivée (*f.*)
tu es arrivé (*m.*)/arrivée (*f.*)
il est arrivé
elle est arrivée
nous sommes arrivés (*m.pl.*)/arrivées (*f.pl.*)
vous êtes arrivés (*m.pl.*)/arrivées (*f.pl.*)
ils sont arrivés (*m.pl.*)
elles sont arrivées (*f.pl.*)

Notice the **-e** in the feminine forms of the past participle, for example, **je suis arrivée**. Also notice the **-s** in the **nous** form: **nous sommes arrivés**. This tells us that the past participle agrees in gender (feminine/masculine) and number (singular/plural) with the subject of the sentence.

Past participles

To form the past participle of a regular verb, drop the **-er/-ir/-re** ending from the infinitive of the verb, then add the endings **é**, **i**, and **u.**

parl-er	parl	é	**parlé**
fin-ir	fin	+ i	**fini**
vend-re	vend	u	**vendu**

Not all French verbs are regular; irregular verbs form their past participle differently. The most obvious exceptions are verbs like the following.

ouvrir ("to open")	ouvert
couvrir ("to cover")	couvert
mettre ("to put," "to wear," "to set")	mis
prendre ("to take")	pris

Some past participles are completely irregular.

faire ("to do," "to make")	fait
être ("to be")	été
avoir ("to have")	eu
boire ("to drink")	bu
vouloir ("to want," "to wish")	voulu
devoir ("to have to," "must")	dû
pouvoir ("to be able to," "can")	pu

Les prépositions · *Prepositions*

à (à la, à l'), en, au, aux ("to," "at")

These prepositions are used to indicate a place we are going to. They also indicate the way, the means, or the purpose of an action.

Note that à may be used with a definite article: le, la, l', les. In such cases, à + le contracts to au, and à + les contracts to aux.

À and à la indicate direction; they are used before the name of a city or the name of a place that is feminine.

à Paris, à New York, à Dijon	*in Paris, in New York, in Dijon*
à la bibliothèque	*at/to the library*
à la maison	*at/to the house*

For provinces, states, countries, and continents, use the following prepositions.

en *before a feminine noun (ending in -e) (for example,* en France; EXCEPTION: au Mexique)

au *before a masculine noun (ending in any vowel but -e or a consonant)* (*for example,* au Canada, au Brésil)

aux *before all plural nouns (for example,* aux États-Unis)

EXCEPTIONS: en Israël, en Iran, en Iraq

Although these nouns end in a consonant (and are therefore considered masculine), they use en instead of au because they start with a vowel. French tries to avoid having two vowel sounds next to one another.

pour

The preposition pour ("to," "for," "in order to") is followed by the infinitive of a verb of action.

pour manger	*to eat/in order to eat*
pour parler	*to speak/in order to speak*
pour dormir	*to sleep/in order to sleep*
Nous allons au restaurant pour manger.	*We are going to the restaurant to eat.*
Nous apprenons le français pour parler avec nos amis canadiens.	*We are learning French in order to speak with our Canadian friends.*
Nous allons à l'hôtel pour dormir.	*We are going to the hotel to sleep.*

Expressions utiles · *Useful expressions*

S'il vous plaît. ⎫ Je vous en prie. ⎭	*Please.*
Merci.	*Thanks.*
De rien. ⎫ À votre service. ⎭	*It's nothing., Don't mention it., You're welcome.*

Quelle heure est-il?   *What time is it?*

Où se trouve _____, s'il vous plaît?   *Where is _____, please?*

J'aimerais _____, ⎫ Je voudrais _____, ⎬ s'il vous plait. Nous voudrions _____, ⎭	*I would like _____,* ⎫ *I would like _____,* ⎬ *please.* *We would like _____,* ⎭

Au revoir!	*Good-bye!*
A bientôt!	*See you soon!*
A plus tard!	*See you later!*
Combien c'est?	*How much is it?*
Attention!	*Watch it! Be careful!*
Bonne chance!	*Good luck!*

Guide de prononciation · *Pronunciation guide*

Although French uses the same alphabet as English, the name of the individual letters frequently sounds quite different. In each chapter you will find a brief section, "How to make it sound French," to help you. Learn these tips one by one.

Accents and symbols

Accents and symbols are an important part of the spelling of French words. Their use can indicate a difference in pronunciation or of meaning between two words of otherwise identical spelling. Most of them were not introduced into the language until the sixteenth century.

The acute accent (´) occurs only over the letter **e**, changing its sound from **e** to **é**. It generally replaces the **s** that occurred in Old French.

escole → école ("school")

The grave accent (`) most often occurs with **e**, lengthening its sound.

le père ("father")
la mère ("mother")
le frère ("brother")

When the grave accent occurs over **a** or **u**, it changes the meaning of the word.

La fille est là. *The girl is there.*
Où allez-vous à Paris **ou** à Lille? *Where are you going, to Paris or Lille?*

The circumflex accent (ˆ) is found over the vowels **a, e, i, o, u.** It generally replaces the **s** of Old French. Interestingly, the **s** has survived in many of the corresponding English words.

la bête ("beast")   la forêt ("forest")
la côte ("coast")   l'hôtel ("hotel," "hostel")

The diaeresis (¨) is placed over the vowels **e, i, o, u** to indicate that the preceding vowel must be pronounced separately.

Noël ("Christmas")
la faïence ("earthenware," "pottery")

The cedilla (¸) is the symbol placed under the letter **c** to indicate that the **c** must be pronounced as an **s**. The cedilla originated in the sixteenth century, when the letter **s** was placed under or over the **c** to indicate the change in sound.

les Français ("the French")

Intonation

As you speak, the natural rise and fall of your voice, known as intonation, reflects your meaning. Intonation is the music of the language.

When speaking, the French have a tendency to raise their voice slightly and then let it fall back to the starting pitch at the beginning of the next phrase or sentence. Think of it as waves singing as they wash on and off the shore.

The range between low pitch and high pitch is much greater in French than it is in spoken English.

Lexique français-anglais

Italic numbers refer to the chapter in which the word or expression is introduced.

à at; in; to *1*
aboyer to bark *8*
l'abricot (*m.*) apricot *2*
l'accord
  d'accord all right, okay *6*
acheter to buy *2*
actif(-ive) active *3*
l'action
  le film d'action action film *2*
l'addition (*f.*) check, bill *4*
adieu good-bye (Switzerland, Canada) *1*
adorer to love; to idolize *2*
l'adresse (*f.*) address *3*
l'aéroport (*m.*) airport *4*
africain(e) African *1*
l'âge (*m.*) age *3*
  Quel âge as-tu? How old are you? *3*
l'agence de voyages (*f.*) travel agency *8*
agressif(-ive) aggressive *3*
aider to help *5*
aimable kind, friendly *3*
aimer to like; to love *2*
ainsi que as well as *9*
alerte alert *3*
l'Algérie (*f.*) Algeria *5*
algérien(ne) Algerian *3*
aller to go *2*
  aller aux toilettes to go to the bathroom/lavatory *4*
  aller et retour round-trip ticket *8*
  Comment allez-vous? How are you? (*formal*) *1*
allumer to light *9*

alors then *2*
ambitieux(-euse) ambitious *3*
américain(e) American *1*
l'ami (*m.*) friend *1*
l'amie (*f.*) friend *1*
l'amour (*m.*) love *1*
amoureux(-euse) in love *3*
l'ampoule (*f.*) lightbulb *5*
l'an
  le jour de l'An New Year's Day *5*
l'ananas (*m.*) pineapple *4*
anglais(e) English *3*
l'année (*f.*) year *3*
l'anniversaire (*m.*) birthday *7*
l'antiquaire (*m.*) antique store *4*
août August *5*
l'apéritif (*m.*) aperitif, before-dinner drink *4*
l'appel (*m.*) phone call *5*
appeler to call *1*
  s'appeler to be called/named *1*
  je m'appelle _____ my name is _____ *1*
  Comment vous appelez-vous? What is your name? *1*
apprécier to appreciate *9*
apprendre to learn *4*
l'après-midi (*m.*) afternoon *2*
l'arrivée (*f.*) arrival *7*
arriver to arrive *4*
assez enough, sufficiently *3*
l'assiette (*f.*) plate, bowl *6*
assister à to attend (an event) *4*
l'Assomption (*f.*) Assumption Day (*August 15*) *5*

astucieux(-euse) astute, resourceful *3*
attendre to wait for *7*
attentif(-ive) attentive *3*
aujourd'hui today *8*
australien(ne) Australian *7*
l'autobus (*m.*) bus *6*
automatique
   la voiture automatique car with automatic transmission *8*
l'automne (*m.*) fall, autumn *2*
l'autoroute (*f.*) highway *7*
autre other *8*
l'avance
   en avance early *3*
avec with *2*
aventureux(-euse) adventurous *3*
avertir to warn *6*
l'avion (*m.*) plane *5*
avoir to have *3*
   avoir besoin de/d' to need *5*
   avoir chaud to be warm *3*
   avoir de la chance to be lucky *3*
   avoir faim to be hungry *3*
   avoir froid to be cold *3*
   avoir peur to be afraid *3*
   avoir rendez-vous to have an appointment *3*
   avoir soif to be thirsty *3*
   avoir sommeil to be tired/sleepy *3*
avril April *5*

la baignoire bathtub *5*
le bain
   la salle de bains bathroom *5*
   la serviette de bain bath towel *5*
la banane banana *4*
la bande dessinée cartoon, comic strip *3*
la banque bank *5*
le bar bar *5*
le base-ball baseball *2*
le basket basketball *2*
beau
   il fait beau it is nice (weather) *2*
beaucoup very much *2*
beaucoup (de) much, many, a lot *5*
le beau-frère brother-in-law *7*
le beau-père father-in-law *7*

les beaux-parents parents-in-law, in-laws *7*
la belle-fille daughter-in-law *6*
la belle-mère mother-in-law *7*
la belle-sœur sister-in-law *7*
ben (*slang for* **bien**) well *7*
le besoin
   avoir besoin de/d' to need *5*
la bibliothèque library *4*
la bicyclette bicycle *2*
bien well *1*
   bien cuit(e) extremely well done (*meat*) *9*
   bien fait ripe (*cheese*) *9*
   bien frais fresh (*cheese*) *9*
bientôt soon *2*
   à bientôt see you soon *1*
la bière beer *4*
   la bière pression draft beer *4*
la bijouterie jewelry store *9*
le billet ticket *2*
   le billet de loterie lottery ticket *5*
   le billet ouvert open ticket (*train*) *8*
le bisou kiss (*colloquial*) *4*
   faire un bisou to give a kiss *4*
blanc/blanche white *4*
bleu(e) blue *8*; very rare (*close to raw; meat*) *9*
blond(e) blond(e) *3*
une blonde pale ale, lager *4*
le bœuf beef *6*
le/les bois wood, woods, grove *3*
la boisson drink, beverage *4*
bon/bonne good *2*
   bon marché cheap, inexpensive *5*
   Bonne journée! Have a nice day! *5*
   bonne nuit good night *1*
le bonbon candy *3*
bonjour hello; good morning; good afternoon *1*
bonsoir hello; good evening; good-bye *1*
la boucherie butcher's shop *9*
la boulangerie bakery *9*
la Bourgogne Burgundy *9*
bourguignon(ne) Burgundian *6*
la bouteille bottle *2*
la boutique de vêtements clothing store *9*

le Brésil Brazil 5
le brigand robber 9
la brosse à dents toothbrush 5
le brouillard fog 2
la brume mist 2
une brune dark/stout beer 4
le bureau desk; office 2
  le bureau de tabac tobacco shop 5
le bus bus 3

ça that 6
  ça fait it costs, it is 4
  Ça ne fait rien. It does not matter. 4
  Ça va? How are you? (*familiar*) 1
  ça vaut la peine de it is worth the trouble/bother to 9
  ça vaut le coup it is worth it 9
le café
  le café crème coffee with milk/cream 4
  le café noir black coffee 4
  la cuillère à café teaspoon 6
le cahier notebook 2
la calculatrice calculator 2
calme calm 3
la calorie calorie 8
la campagne countryside 6
canadien(ne) Canadian 3
le canard duck 6
le cappuccino cappuccino 2
car because 8
la carafe carafe, decanter 4
cartable schoolbag 2
la carte map; menu; card 3
  la carte de crédit credit card 3
  la carte d'identité ID card 9
la cartouche cartridge 2
la cassette cassette 2
le cassis blackcurrant 4
la cathédrale cathedral 7
la cave cellar, basement 8
  la cave à vin wine cellar 8
la caverne cavern, cave 9
ce/cette this, that 5
célèbre famous 6
la cendre ash 9
cent one hundred 5
la cerise cherry 3

ces these, those 8
c'est it is 3
  c'est-à-dire that is to say 6
  C'est combien? How much is it? 4
la chaise chair 5
chaleureux(-euse) warm-hearted, warm 3
la chambre hotel room; room 5
  la chambre climatisée air-conditioned room 5
  la chambre double double room 5
  la chambre simple single room 5
le champagne champagne 4
la chance
  avoir de la chance to be lucky 3
la charcuterie (pork) butcher's shop 9
charmant(e) charming 3
le chat cat 6
chaud(e) hot, warm 2
  avoir chaud to be warm 3
  l'eau chaude (*f.*) hot water 5
  il fait chaud it is warm (weather) 2
la chaussée
  le rez-de-chaussée ground floor 7
la chaussure shoe 7
cher/chère expensive 5
le chercheur/la chercheuse research scientist 9
le chéri/la chérie
  mon chéri darling 1
  ma chérie darling 1
les cheveux (*m.pl.*) hair 3
  le séchoir à cheveux hair dryer 5
le chèvre goat cheese 9
la chèvre goat 9
chez at the home of 9
  Faites comme chez vous. Make yourself at home. 4
le chien dog 8
chinois(e) Chinese 3
le chocolat chocolate 2
choisir to choose 2
Chut! Hush! 9
le cidre cider 7
la cigarette cigarette 7
le cinéma cinema, film 2
cinq five 3

cinquante fifty 4
cinquième fifth 7
le cirque circus 6
le citron lemon 4
  le citron pressé lemonade, fresh lemon juice 4
la classe class 2
  la classe économique coach class (*airplane*) 6
  la première classe first class (*train, airplane*) 6
le classeur binder 2
classique classical 2
la clé key 5
climatiser
  la chambre climatisée air-conditioned room 5
le club club 6
le coca-cola coke, Coca-Cola 4
le cocktail cocktail 6
combien
  C'est combien? How much is it? 4
commander to order 2
comme as, like 3
  comme ci comme ça so-so 1
  Faites comme chez vous. Make yourself at home. 4
commencer to start 2
comment how 8
  Comment allez-vous? How are you? (*formal*) 1
  Comment cela? How come?, What? 5
  Comment vous appelez-vous? What is your name? 1
la communication phone call; communication 5
complet/complète full 5
composter to punch (a ticket) 8
la compote compote (*fruit*) 6
  en compote crushed to pulp (*fruit*) 6
comprendre to understand 4
compter to count 4
le concert concert 3
la confirmation confirmation 5
le congé leave; vacation 7
  en congé on leave; on vacation 7
le congrès convention 4

connaître to know, to be familiar with 8
construire to build 7
content(e) happy, content 3
le coq rooster 1
le côté side 5
  à côté de next to 6
  le côté cour overlooking the courtyard 5
  le côté rue overlooking the street 5
le couloir corridor, hall 7
courageux(-euse) courageous 3
la course race; errand 6
  faire des courses to go shopping 9
court(e) short (*not for people*) 3
le cousin/la cousine cousin 7
le couteau knife 6
le couvert place setting 6
la couverture blanket 5
le crayon pencil 2
la crème cream 2
  la crème brûlée crème brûlée (*a custard topped with caramelized sugar*) 2
  le café crème coffee with milk/cream 4
la crémerie dairy (store) 9
la crêpe crêpe; pancake 2
la crevette shrimp 6
le criminel criminal 6
le croissant croissant 2
le croque-monsieur grilled ham-and-cheese sandwich 6
le cru first-rate vineyard 9
cru(e) raw (*like steak tartare*) 9
les crudités (*f.pl.*) raw vegetables 6
cubain(e) Cuban 3
cueillir to pick up; to gather 3
la cuillère, la cuiller spoon 6
  la cuillère à café teaspoon 6
  la cuillère à dessert dessertspoon 6
  la cuillère à soupe tablespoon 6
  la petite cuillère dessertspoon 6
la cuisine
  faire la cuisine to cook 9
cuisiner to cook 6
cuit(e)
  bien cuit(e) extremely well done (*meat*) 9

d'abord first *4*
d'accord okay, all right *4*
dangereux(-euse) dangerous *3*
de from, of *1*
le décalage horaire jet lag *4*
décembre December *5*
la décision decision *7*
dehors outside *9*
le déjeuner lunch *6*
  le petit déjeuner breakfast *6*
délicieux(-euse) delicious *2*
demain tomorrow *5*
  à demain see you tomorrow *1*
demander to ask (for) *4*
demi(e) half *4*
le demi-frère stepbrother,
    half brother *7*
la demi-sœur stepsister, half sister *7*
la dent
  la brosse à dents toothbrush *5*
le dentifrice toothpaste *5*
le dentiste dentist *1*
le départ departure *8*
derrière behind *6*
descendre to go down, to come down
    7
désirer to want, to wish *4*
désolé(e) sorry *5*
le dessert dessert *2*
  la cuillère à dessert dessertspoon *6*
détester to dislike, to detest *2*
deux two *3*
deuxième second *7*
devant in front of *6*
devenir to become *9*
le devoir homework *6*
devoir + *noun* to owe *5*
devoir + *verb* to have to, must *5*
difficile difficult *7*
dimanche Sunday *5*
le dîner dinner *6*
dire to tell, to say *7*
  c'est-à-dire that is to say *6*
  vouloir dire to mean *7*
la direction direction *9*
le discours speech *2*
divorcé(e) divorced *7*
dix ten *3*
dix-huit eighteen *4*

dixième tenth *7*
dix-neuf nineteen *4*
dix-sept seventeen *4*
le docteur doctor *1*
la doctoresse doctor (*female*) *6*
le domaine estate *9*
donc therefore, then, hence *8*
donner sur to open onto, to face
    onto *5*
dormir to sleep *6*
double
  la chambre double double room *5*
la douche shower *5*
  prendre une douche to take a
    shower *5*
douze twelve *3*
le drap bedsheet *5*
droit(e) straight *3*
  tout droit straight ahead *7*
  à droite to the right *7*

l'eau (*f.*) water *4*
  l'eau chaude (*f.*) hot water *5*
  l'eau froide (*f.*) cold water *5*
  l'eau gazeuse (*f.*) sparkling mineral
    water (*carbonated*) *4*
  l'eau minérale (*f.*) mineral water *4*
  l'eau pétillante (*f.*) sparkling
    mineral water (*carbonated*) *4*
  l'eau plate (*f.*) still mineral water
    (*noncarbonated*) *4*
économique economical *5*
  la classe économique coach class
    (*airplane*) *6*
écouter to listen (to) *2*
les effets de toilette (*m.pl.*) toiletries
    5
égoïste selfish *3*
eh hey *2*
  eh bien well *2*
l'électricien(ne) electrician *1*
l'électroménager (*m.*) household
    appliance *9*
elle she, it (*f.*), her, herself *1*
elles they (*f.*), them, themselves *1*
l'embrayage (*m.*) clutch (car) *8*
  la voiture à embrayage car with
    manual transmission *8*
émotif(-ive) emotional *3*

en in; to *2*

  en avance early *3*

  en compote crushed to pulp (*fruit*) *6*

  en face de in front of *6*

  en fleurs blooming, in bloom *2*

  en particulier particularly *9*

enchanté(e) delighted *1*

encore still, more, again, yet *5*

  encore une fois one more time *5*

les enfants (*m.pl.*) children *7*

enfin finally *4*

énorme huge *3*

ensemble together *2*

ensuite then, next, afterward *4*

entendre to hear *7*

entièrement totally, entirely *6*

entre between *6*

entrer to enter *9*

l'épicerie (*f.*) grocer's, grocery store *9*

l'escargot (*m.*) snail *6*

l'escrime (*f.*) fencing *4*

espagnol(e) Spanish *3*

l'esprit (*m.*) spirit; mind *3*

et and *1*

l'étage (*m.*) floor *7*

l'été (*m.*) summer *2*

étranger(-ère) foreign *8*

être to be *1*

  être en congé to be off (work), to be on leave *7*

  être en pleine forme to feel great *3*

  être en retard to be late *3*

  être en train de to be in the act of *9*

  être pressé(e) to be in a hurry *3*

  être sûr(e) to be sure/certain *3*

  Vous êtes d'où? Where do you come from? *1*

l'étude (*f.*) study *3*

l'étudiant (*m.*) student *1*

l'étudiante (*f.*) student *1*

étudier to study *2*

européen(ne) European *1*

eux they, them, themselves *4*

excellent(e) excellent *2*

excusez-moi excuse me, sorry *1*

l'expresso (*m.*) espresso *4*

la face

  en face de in front of *6*

la faim

  avoir faim to be hungry *3*

  mourir de faim to starve *9*

faire to do; to make *2*

  bien fait ripe (*cheese*) *9*

  Ça ne fait rien. It does not matter. *4*

  faire des courses to go shopping *9*

  faire du shopping to go shopping *4*

  faire du sport to play (*practice*) a sport *4*

  faire la cuisine to cook *9*

  faire la lessive to do (the) laundry *9*

  faire la sieste to take a nap *4*

  faire la vaisselle to do the dishes *9*

  faire le ménage to clean the house *9*

  faire le mort to play dead *9*

  faire un bisou to give a kiss *4*

  faire un gâteau to bake a cake *4*

  faire un tour to go for a ride *4*

  faire une promenade to take a walk *4*

  faire vite to hurry *9*

  Faites comme chez vous. Make yourself at home. *4*

  Faites le plein! Fill up the tank! *4*

  il fait beau it is nice (weather) *2*

  il fait chaud it is warm (weather) *2*

  il fait du vent it is windy *2*

  il fait frais it is cool (weather) *2*

  il fait froid it is cold (weather) *2*

  il fait mauvais it is bad (weather) *2*

  n'est plus à faire need not be made/drawn *6*

  ne vous en faites pas do not worry *4*

  Qu'est-ce que ça peut faire? What does it matter? *8*

  Quel temps fait-il? What is the weather like? *2*

  tout à fait absolutely, completely *6*

  trop fait overripe (*cheese*) *9*

falloir
  a-t-il fallu? did it take?, did it require? 7
la famille family 7
fatigué(e) tired 1
le fauteuil armchair 5
la femme woman; wife 4
la fenêtre window 5
fermé(e) closed 7
le festival festival, celebration 5
la fête celebration, party; feast day 5
la feuille sheet (*of paper*) 2
février February 5
la fille girl 2; daughter 7
le film d'action action film 2
le fils son 7
finir to finish 6
la fleur flower 2
  en fleurs blooming, in bloom 2
la fois
  encore une fois one more time 5
le fond back, far end; background 7
le football soccer 4
fort(e) strong 3
fou/folle mad, crazy 3
la fourchette fork 6
frais
  bien frais fresh; young (*cheese*) 9
  il fait frais it is cool (weather) 2
  trop frais too fresh (*cheese*) 9
la fraise strawberry 4
la framboise raspberry 4
le français French (*language*) 2
le Français/la Française French (*person*) 2
la France France 2
le frère brother 7
froid(e) cold 2
  avoir froid to be cold 3
  l'eau froide (*f.*) cold water 5
  il fait froid it is cold (weather) 2
le fromage cheese 4
le fruit
  la salade de fruits fruit salad 6
  la tarte aux fruits fruit pie 2
la fumée smoke 9

fumer to smoke 5
furieux(-euse) furious 3

le gant de toilette facecloth, washcloth 5
le garçon boy; waiter 2
la gare train station 4
le gâteau cake 2
  faire un gâteau to bake a cake 4
la gauche
  à gauche to the left 7
gazeux(-euse)
  l'eau gazeuse (*f.*) sparkling mineral water (*carbonated*) 4
le gendre son-in-law 7
général(e)
  en général in general 6
généreux(-euse) generous 3
Genève Geneva 4
la glace ice cream; ice 6
glacé(e) icy; iced 6
gourmand(e) gourmand (*food-loving*) 6
grand(e) big; tall; great 3
grandir to grow 6
la grand-mère grandmother 7
le grand-père grandfather 7
les grands-parents (*m.pl.*) grandparents 7
grossir to gain weight 6
la grotte cave, grotto 8
la guitare guitar 2
la gymnastique gymnastics; exercise 6

habiter to live (somewhere) 2
haut(e) high 3
le héros hero 3
l'heure (*f.*) hour; time 3
  à tout à l'heure see you later 1
  Quelle heure est-il? What time is it? 3
heureux(-euse) happy 3
hier yesterday 7
l'hirondelle (*f.*) swallow (*bird*) 2
historique historic 2
l'hiver (*m.*) winter 2

le homard lobster 3
l'homme (*m.*) man 3
horaire
le décalage horaire jet lag 4
le hors-d'œuvre appetizer, hors d'oeuvre 6
l'hôtel (*m.*) hotel 3
le maître d'hôtel headwaiter, maître d' 6
huit eight 3
huitième eighth 7

ici
n'était pas ici was not here 7
par ici this way, over here 6
idéaliste idealistic 3
l'idée (*f.*) idea 2
il he, it (*m.*) 1
ils they (*m.*) 1
impatient(e) impatient, eager 3
l'imperméable (*m.*) raincoat 9
l'important (*m.*) the important thing 8
impossible impossible 5
impulsif(-ive) impulsive 3
indépendant(e) independent 3
l'indicatif (*m.*) area code (*telephone*) 5
un instant a minute, a moment 4
intelligent(e) intelligent 3
intéressant(e) interesting 3
l'Internet (*m.*) Internet 5
l'interrupteur (*m.*) light switch 5
l'invité(e) guest 6
inviter to invite 6
irritable irritable 3
l'Italie (*f.*) Italy 1
italien(ne) Italian (*person*) 3
ivre drunk 9

le jambon ham 4
janvier January 5
japonais(e) Japanese 3
le jardin garden 6
jaune yellow 3
je I 1
jeudi Thursday 5
la jeunesse youth 7
jouer to play 2

le jour day 5
le jour de l'An New Year's Day 5
le jour férié holiday 5
le plat du jour daily special (*restaurant*) 3
le/la journaliste journalist 1
la journée day, daytime 5
Bonne journée! Have a nice day! 5
le juge judge 6
juillet July 5
juin June 5
le jus juice 4
jusque as far as 8

le karaté karate 4
le kir kir (aperitif) 4

lacustre lakeside (*village or home*) 9
le lait milk 4
le lait-fraise strawberry milkshake 4
le lapin rabbit 6
la laverie automatique laundromat 9
la lessive
faire la lessive to do (the) laundry 9
leur/leurs their 7
se lever to stand up, to get up 9
la librairie bookstore 9
le lit bed 5
le livre book 2
la location rental 8
loin de far (from) 6
Londres London 4
long(ue) long 3
longtemps for a long time 9
la loterie
le billet de loterie lottery ticket 5
louer to rent 8
lourd(e) heavy 3
lundi Monday 5
la lune moon 6

Madame, Mesdames Mrs., madam (mesdames) 1
Mademoiselle miss 1
magique magical 6
magnifique magnificent, splendid, superb 9

mai May *5*
maigrir to lose weight *6*
la main hand *9*
maintenant now *8*
mais but *3*
la maison house *6*
le maître d'hôtel headwaiter,
   maître d' *6*
mal badly *1*
   pas mal not bad *1*
malade sick, ill *3*
malheureux(-euse) unhappy *3*
la maman mama, mom, mommy *1*
la Manche English Channel *6*
manger to eat *2*
le manteau de pluie raincoat *9*
le marchand de vin wine merchant *9*
le marché
   bon marché cheap, inexpensive *5*
marcher to walk; to work, to function
   2
le mari husband *7*
le Maroc Morocco *6*
le marronnier chestnut tree *2*
mars March *5*
le match match (*sports*) *2*
le matin morning *2*
la matinée morning, the morning
   hours *8*
mauvais(e) bad *7*
   il fait mauvais it is bad (weather) *2*
le/la mécanicien(ne) mechanic *1*
la médecine medicine (*field of study*)
   1
médical(e) medical *4*
Melba
   la pêche Melba peach Melba
   (*dessert*) *2*
le ménage
   faire le ménage to clean the house
   9
la menthe mint *4*
la mer sea *2*
merci thank you *1*
mercredi Wednesday *5*
la mère mother *7*
la merveille
   le pays des merveilles wonderland
   6

Mesdemoiselles misses, young ladies
   1
Messieurs gentlemen *1*
Messieurs-dames ladies and
   gentlemen *1*
le métro subway *7*
mettre to put (on) *9*
mexicain(e) Mexican *3*
miauler to meow *8*
midi midday, noon *4*
   l'après-midi (*m.*) afternoon *2*
le milieu
   au milieu de in the middle of *6*
mille one thousand *5*
minéral(e)
   l'eau minérale (*f.*) mineral water
   4
minuit midnight *4*
le mobile cell phone *5*
moderne modern *3*
moi I, myself (*for my part*) *2*
   moi aussi so do I *2*
   moi non plus neither do I *6*
le mois month *5*
mon/ma/mes my *1*
mondial(e) worldwide *6*
Monsieur Mr., sir *1*
monter to get in; to go up *4*
le monument monument *2*
le mort
   faire le mort to play dead *9*
la mortadelle mortadella (*cold cut*)
   9
Moscou Moscow *4*
mourir to die *9*
   mourir de faim to starve *9*
la mousse au chocolat chocolate
   mousse *2*
la moustache mustache *3*
la moutarde mustard *6*
musclé(e) muscular *3*
le musée museum *1*
la musique music *7*

nager to swim *2*
naître to be born *9*
la nappe tablecloth *6*
la natation swimming *4*
la nature nature *2*

neiger to snow *2*
neuf nine *3*
neuf/neuve new, brand-new *3*
neuvième ninth *7*
le neveu nephew *7*
la nièce niece *7*
le Noël Christmas *5*
noir(e) black *8*
  le café noir black coffee *4*
le nom name *5*
non no *1*
  non plus neither *6*
notre/nos our *7*
nous we, us, ourselves *1*
la Nouvelle-Orléans New Orleans *4*
novembre November *5*
la nuit night *2*
  bonne nuit good night *1*
le numéro number *5*

obéir to obey *5*
occupé(e) busy *4*
octobre October *5*
l'oignon (*m.*) onion *6*
l'omelette (*f.*) omelet *6*
l'oncle (*m.*) uncle *7*
onze eleven *3*
optimiste optimistic *3*
l'orage (*m.*) storm *2*
l'orange (*f.*) orange *2*
l'ordinateur (*m.*) computer *2*
l'oreiller (*m.*) pillow *5*
ou or *2*
où where *1*
  Vous êtes d'où? Where do you
    come from? *1*
oublier to forget *9*
oui yes *2*
ouvert(e) open, opened *7*
  le billet ouvert open ticket (*train*) *8*

le pain bread *9*
le pamplemousse grapefruit *4*
le panier basket *9*
le papa daddy, dad *1*
le papier hygiénique toilet paper *5*
Pâques Easter *5*
par ici this way, over here *6*
le parapluie umbrella *6*

parce que because *5*
pardon excuse me, sorry *1*
les parents (*m.pl.*) parents; relatives
  7
le parfum perfume *7*
parisien(ne) Parisian *4*
parler to speak, to talk *2*
la parole spoken word *9*
particulier(-ière)
  en particulier particularly *9*
partir to leave *6*
le passant/la passante passerby *7*
le passeport passport *5*
passer to pass *4*
  passer par to go through; to make
    a stop at *8*
la pâtisserie pastry *2*
payer to pay *4*
le pays country, nation *7*
  le pays des merveilles wonderland
    6
  le vin du pays local wine *9*
la pêche Melba peach Melba (*dessert*)
  2
la peine
  ça vaut la peine de it is worth the
    trouble/bother to *9*
la peinture painting *9*
  la peinture rupestre rock painting
    9
penser to think *7*
la Pentecôte Whitsuntide, Pentecost
  5
perdre to lose *7*
le père father *7*
permettez-moi allow me *1*
la personne person *3*
pétillant(e)
  l'eau pétillante (*f.*) sparkling
    mineral water (*carbonated*) *4*
petit(e) small *3*
  le petit déjeuner breakfast *6*
  la petite cuillère dessertspoon *6*
la petite-fille granddaughter *7*
le petit-fils grandson *7*
un peu a little *2*
la peur
  avoir peur to be afraid *3*
peut-être perhaps, maybe *9*

je peux I can *5*
la pharmacie pharmacy, drugstore *9*
la photo photo *4*
photographier to photograph *8*
le pique-nique picnic *9*
la pizza pizza *4*
la plage beach *2*
plaire
  s'il vous plaît (*pl. and formal sing.*)
    please *4*
  s'il te plaît (*familiar sing.*) please
    4
le plaisir pleasure *2*
la planète planet *5*
le plat
  le plat du jour daily special *3*
  le plat principal main dish *6*
plat(e)
  l'eau plate (*f.*) still mineral water
    (*noncarbonated*) *4*
le plein
  Faites le plein! Fill up the tank! *4*
plein(e)
  être en pleine forme to feel great
    3
pleurer to cry, to weep *9*
pleuvoir to rain *2*
  il pleut it rains, it's raining *2*
le plombier plumber *1*
la pluie
  le manteau de pluie raincoat *9*
plus more *5*
  moi non plus neither do I *6*
  n'est plus à faire need not be
    made/drawn *6*
  non plus neither *6*
la poire pear *4*
le poisson fish *6*
le poivre pepper *6*
la pomme apple *4*
la porcelaine de Limoges Limoges
  china *7*
la porte door *5*
positif(-ive) positive *3*
la possibilité possibility *3*
le poste position, job *3*
la poste post office *9*
le pourboire tip (*in a restaurant*) *4*
Pourquoi pas? Why not? *2*

pouvoir to be able to, can *5*
préféré(e) preferred *2*
préférer to prefer *8*
la préhistoire prehistory *8*
la première classe first class (*train,*
  airplane) *6*
prendre to take *4*
  prendre une douche to take a
    shower *5*
près de near *6*
la présentation introduction *1*
présenter to introduce *1*
le président/la présidente president
  2
pressé(e)
  le citron pressé lemonade, fresh
    lemon juice *4*
  être pressé(e) to be in a hurry *3*
  je suis pressé(e) I am in a hurry
    1
prétendre to claim *7*
le printemps spring *2*
Prisunic *a popular French department*
  store *9*
le problème problem *5*
prochain(e) next *3*
le professeur teacher, professor *1*
la promenade
  faire une promenade to take a walk
    4
se promener to stroll, to walk
  leisurely *7*
prudent(e) cautious *3*
psychanalytique psychoanalytical *3*
punir to punish *6*

qu'est-ce que/qu'? what? *2*
Qu'est-ce que ça peut faire? What
  does it matter? *8*
Qu'est-ce que c'est? What is it? *3*
qu'est-ce qui y'a? what is there? *7*
quarante forty *4*
le quart
  et quart quarter past (*time*) *4*
  moins le quart quarter to (*time*) *4*
quatorze fourteen *4*
quatre four *3*
quatre-vingt-dix ninety *5*
quatre-vingts eighty *5*

quatrième fourth *7*
quel(le) what, which *2*
 Quel âge as-tu? How old are you? *3*
 Quel temps fait-il? What is the weather like? *2*
 Quelle heure est-il? What time is it? *3*
quelquefois sometimes *3*
quelques some, a few, any *9*
qui who, which, that *3*
Qui c'est? Who is he/she? *3*
Qui est-ce? Who is he/she? *3*
Qui est-ce que c'est? Who is he/she? *3*
quinze fifteen *4*
quitter
 Ne me quitte pas. Don't leave me. *1*
quoi what *6*

la randonnée excursion *8*
rapide fast *8*
le rasoir razor *5*
la réception reception desk *5*
le/la réceptionniste receptionist *1*
réfléchir to ponder, to reflect *6*
regarder to look (at) *2*
le régime diet *8*
la région region, area *8*
la relâche break, no performance *7*
remplir to fill *6*
le rendez-vous appointment, meeting; date *7*
 avoir rendez-vous to have an appointment *3*
rendre to give up, to give back *7*
la renommée reputation *6*
rentrer to return, to come back *8*
le repas meal *6*
le repassage ironing *6*
répondre to answer *7*
représenter to represent *3*
la république republic *9*
la réservation reservation *3*
réserver to reserve *2*
ressembler à to look like *7*
le restaurant restaurant *2*
 le wagon-restaurant dining car *9*

rester to stay, to remain *4*
le retard
 être en retard to be late *3*
le retour return *8*
 aller et retour round-trip ticket *8*
réussir to succeed *6*
revenir to come back *9*
rêver to dream *2*
revoir
 au revoir good-bye, see you later *1*
le rez-de-chaussée ground floor *7*
riche wealthy, rich *7*
rien nothing *7*
 De rien. Don't mention it., You are welcome. *1*
le rond ring *9*
rouge red *3*
 toutes rouges all red *3*
la route road *2*
la rue street *7*
 le côté rue overlooking the street *5*

le sac schoolbag, bag *2*
saignant(e) medium rare (*meat*) *9*
Sainte-Hélène Saint Helena (*island*) *9*
la salade salad *2*
 la salade de fruits fruit salad *6*
la salle de bains bathroom *5*
salut hi *1*
samedi Saturday *5*
le sandwich sandwich *4*
sans without *5*
saoul(e) drunk *9*
la sauce sauce; salad dressing *4*
la saucisse sausage *4*
le saucisson sec salami *4*
le sauna sauna *5*
savoir (je sais) to know (I know) *8*
la savonnette bath soap *5*
le séchoir à cheveux hair dryer *5*
le/la secrétaire secretary *1*
seize sixteen *4*
le sel salt *6*
la semaine week *5*
sept seven *3*
septembre September *5*
septième seventh *7*
seront will be *3*

le serveur waiter 7
la serveuse waitress 6
le service service, duty 7
  à votre service you are welcome 7
la serviette
  la serviette de bain bath towel 5
  la serviette de table napkin 6
  la serviette de toilette hand towel 5
servir to serve 6
seulement only 5
le shopping
  faire du shopping to go shopping 4
s'il te plaît (*familiar sing.*) please 4
s'il vous plaît (*pl. and formal sing.*) please 4
la sieste
  faire la sieste to take a nap 4
simple
  la chambre simple single room 5
sincère sincere 3
la sirène horn, siren 7
six six 3
sixième sixth 7
le ski ski; skiing 2
skier to ski 2
sociable sociable 3
le soda soda 7
la sœur sister 7
la soif
  avoir soif to be thirsty 3
le soir evening 2
la soirée evening (*period of time*) 8
soixante sixty 4
soixante-dix seventy 5
le sommeil
  avoir sommeil to be tired/sleepy 3
son/sa/ses his, her, its 7
le sorbet sherbet 2
la soucoupe saucer 6
la soupe soup 6
  la cuillère à soupe tablespoon 6
sous under 6
les souvenirs-cadeaux (*m.pl.*) gift store 9
souvent often 2
les spaghettis spaghetti 4

le spectacle show, sight 7
la spéléologie speleology, cave exploration 9
le sport
  faire du sport to play (*practice*) a sport 4
sportif(-ive) athletic 3
la stalactite stalactite 9
le stylo ink (ballpoint) pen 2
suédois(e) Swedish 3
suivez-moi follow me 6
le supermarché supermarket 9
sur on 2
sûr(e)
  être sûr(e) to be sure/certain 3
surpris(e) surprised 8
surtout especially, above all 8
  surtout pas especially not 8

le tabac
  le bureau de tabac tobacco shop 5
la table table 2
  la serviette de table napkin 6
la tante aunt 7
tard late 6
  plus tard later 7
la tarte tart, pie 4
  la tarte aux fruits fruit pie 2
la tasse cup 4
le taxi taxi 4
le technicien/la technicienne technician 1
le tee-shirt tee-shirt 7
la télé TV 2
la télécarte phone card 5
le téléphone telephone 3
téléphoner to telephone, to phone 5
la télévision television 2
le temps weather; time 2
  Quel temps fait-il? What is the weather like? 2
le tennis tennis 2
terminer to end 2
la terrasse terrace 1
le TGV (le Train à Grande Vitesse) high-speed train 8
le thé nature tea (*plain*) 4
le théâtre theater 5
timide shy, timid 3

toi you, yourself (*familiar sing.*) *2*
la toilette
  les effets de toilette (*m.pl.*)
  toiletries *5*
  le gant de toilette facecloth,
  washcloth *5*
  la serviette de toilette hand towel
  5
les toilettes (*f.pl.*) toilet *4*
  aller aux toilettes to go to the
  bathroom/lavatory *4*
la tomate tomato *4*
tomber to fall *9*
ton/ta/tes your (*familiar*) *7*
le total total *3*
le tour
  le Tour de France *famous bicycle race
  in July 9*
  faire un tour to go for a ride *4*
la tour tower *4*
le/la touriste tourist *5*
tourner to stir *9*
la Toussaint All Saints' Day *5*
tout(e) all, every *7*
  tout à fait absolutely, completely *6*
  à tout à l'heure see you later *1*
  tout droit straight ahead *7*
  toutes rouges all red *3*
le train train *4*
  le Train à Grande Vitesse (TGV)
  high-speed train *8*
  être en train de to be in the act of
  9
le traiteur gourmet deli *9*
la tranche slice *9*
le travail work *5*
travailler to work *2*
à travers through, across *8*
le traversin bolster (*pillow*) *5*
treize thirteen *4*
trente thirty *4*
trois three *3*
troisième third *7*
trop
  trop fait overripe (*cheese*) *9*
  trop frais too fresh (cheese) *9*
tu you (*familiar sing.*) *1*
la Tunisie Tunisia *5*
tunisien(ne) Tunisian *3*

un one (*number*) *3*
utiliser to use *5*

les vacances (*f.pl.*) vacation, holidays
  3
la vaisselle
  faire la vaisselle to do the dishes
  9
la vanille vanilla *2*
vaniteux(-euse) vain *3*
vendre to sell *7*
vendredi Friday *5*
venir de + *noun* to come from *9*
venir de + *verb* to have just
  accomplished something *9*
le vent
  il fait du vent it is windy *2*
le verglas road ice, black ice *2*
le verre glass *4*
vert(e) green *3*
le/la vétérinaire veterinarian *1*
la victoire victory *5*
le vin wine *4*
  la cave à vin wine cellar *8*
  le marchand de vin wine merchant
  9
  le vin du pays local wine *9*
vingt twenty *4*
visiter to visit (a place) *2*
vite
  faire vite to hurry *9*
la vitesse speed *8*
  le Train à Grande Vitesse (le TGV)
  high-speed train *8*
vive long live *9*
voici here is *2*
  la voici here it (*f.*) is *5*
voilà here is, there is *4*
la voile sailing *4*
voir to see *7*
la voiture car *8*
  la voiture à embrayage car with
  manual transmission *8*
  la voiture automatique car with
  automatic transmission *8*
votre/vos your (*pl. or formal sing.*) *7*
vouloir to want, to wish, to desire to
  5
  vouloir dire to mean *7*

vous you (*pl. or formal sing.*), yourself, yourselves *1*
le voyage trip *2*
  l'agence de voyages (*f.*) travel agency *8*
voyager to travel *2*
le/la voyagiste travel agent *8*

vrai(e) true *4*
vraiment truly, really *9*

le wagon-restaurant dining car *9*
le week-end weekend *6*

zéro zero *3*

Lexique anglais-français

Italic numbers refer to the chapter in which the word or expression is introduced.

a few quelques *9*
a lot beaucoup (de) *5*
a minute un instant *4*
able
  to be able to pouvoir *5*
above all (*especially*) surtout
  8
absolutely tout à fait *6*
across à travers *8*
act
  to be in the act of être en train de
  9
action film le film d'action *2*
active actif(-ive) *3*
address l'adresse (*f.*) *3*
adventurous aventureux(-euse)
  3
afraid
  to be afraid avoir peur *3*
African africain(e) *1*
afternoon l'après-midi (*m.*) *2*
  good afternoon bonjour *1*
afterward ensuite *4*
again encore *5*
age l'âge (*m.*) *3*
aggressive agressif(-ive) *3*
ahead
  straight ahead tout droit *7*
air-conditioned room la chambre
  climatisée *5*
airport l'aéroport (*m.*) *4*
ale
  pale ale une blonde *4*
alert alerte *3*
Algeria l'Algérie (*f.*) *5*
Algerian algérien(ne) *3*

all tout/toute *7*
  all red toutes rouges *3*
  all right d'accord *6*
  All Saints' Day la Toussaint *5*
allow me permettez-moi *1*
ambitious ambitieux(-euse) *3*
American américain(e) *1*
and et *1*
to answer répondre *7*
antique store l'antiquaire (*m.*) *4*
any quelque *9*
aperitif l'apéritif (*m.*) *4*
appetizer le hors-d'œuvre *6*
apple la pomme *4*
appliance
  household appliance
    l'électroménager (*m.*) *9*
appointment le rendez-vous *7*
  to have an appointment avoir
    rendez-vous *3*
to appreciate apprécier *9*
apricot l'abricot (*m.*) *2*
April avril *5*
area la région *8*
area code l'indicatif (*m.*) *5*
armchair le fauteuil *5*
arrival l'arrivée (*f.*) *7*
to arrive arriver *4*
as (*like*) comme *3*
as far as jusque *8*
as well as ainsi que *9*
ash la cendre *9*
to ask (for) demander *4*
Assumption Day (*August 15*)
  l'Assomption (*f.*) *5*
astute astucieux(-euse) *3*

207

at à *1*
athletic sportif(-ive) *3*
to attend assister à *4*
attentive attentif(-ive) *3*
August août *5*
aunt la tante *7*
Australian australien(ne) *7*
autobus l'autobus (*m.*) *6*
automatic car (*car with automatic transmission*) la voiture automatique *8*
autumn l'automne (*m.*) *2*

back (*far end*) le fond *7*
bad mauvais(e) *7*
  it is bad (weather) il fait mauvais *2*
  not bad pas mal *1*
badly mal *1*
bag le sac *3*
to bake a cake faire un gâteau *4*
bakery la boulangerie *9*
ballpoint pen le stylo *2*
banana la banane *4*
bank la banque *5*
bar le bar *5*
to bark aboyer *8*
baseball le base-ball *2*
basket le panier *9*
basketball le basket *2*
bath soap la savonnette *5*
bath towel la serviette de bain *5*
bathroom la salle de bains *5*
  to go to the bathroom/lavatory aller aux toilettes *4*
bathtub la baignoire *5*
to be être *1*
beach la plage *2*
because car *8*; parce que *5*
to become devenir *9*
bed le lit *5*
bedsheet le drap *5*
beef le bœuf *6*
beer la bière *4*
  dark/stout beer une brune *4*
  draft beer la bière pression *4*
  pale ale une blonde *4*
behind derrière *6*
between entre *6*

bicycle la bicyclette *2*
big grand(e) *3*
bill l'addition (*f.*) *4*
binder le classeur *2*
birthday l'anniversaire (*m.*) *7*
black noir(e) *8*
  black coffee le café noir *4*
  black ice le verglas *2*
blackcurrant le cassis *4*
blanket la couverture *5*
blond(e) blond(e) *3*
bloom
  in bloom en fleurs *2*
blue bleu(e) *8*
bolster (*pillow*) le traversin *5*
book le livre *2*
bookstore la librairie *9*
born
  to be born naître *9*
bottle la bouteille *2*
boy le garçon *2*
Brazil le Brésil *5*
bread le pain *9*
break (*no performance*) la relâche *7*
breakfast le petit déjeuner *6*
brother le frère *7*
brother-in-law le beau-frère *7*
to build construire *7*
bulb
  lightbulb l'ampoule (*f.*) *5*
Burgundian bourguignon(ne) *6*
Burgundy la Bourgogne *9*
bus l'autobus (*m.*) *6*; le bus *3*
busy occupé(e) *4*
but mais *3*
butcher's shop la boucherie *9*
  (pork) butcher's shop la charcuterie *9*
to buy acheter *2*

cake le gâteau *2*
  to bake a cake faire un gâteau *4*
calculator la calculatrice *2*
to call appeler *1*
  to be called s'appeler *1*
calm calme *3*
calorie la calorie *8*
can (I can) pouvoir (je peux) *5*
Canadian canadien(ne) *3*

candy le bonbon *3*
cappuccino le cappuccino *2*
car la voiture *8*
　car with automatic transmission
　　la voiture automatique *8*
　car with manual transmission
　　la voiture à embrayage *8*
　dining car le wagon-restaurant *9*
carafe la carafe *4*
carbonated mineral water l'eau
　gazeuse/pétillante (*f.*) *4*
card la carte *3*
　credit card la carte de crédit *3*
　phone card la télécarte *5*
cartoon la bande dessinée *3*
cartridge la cartouche *2*
cassette la cassette *2*
cat le chat *6*
cathedral la cathédrale *7*
cautious prudent(e) *3*
cave la grotte *8*; la caverne *9*
cave exploration la spéléologie *9*
cavern la caverne *9*
celebration la fête *5*
cellar la cave *8*
cell phone le mobile *5*
certain
　to be certain être sûr(e) *3*
chair la chaise *5*
champagne le champagne *4*
channel
　English Channel la Manche *6*
charming charmant(e) *3*
cheap bon marché *5*
check (*restaurant*) l'addition (*f.*) *4*
cheese le fromage *4*
　goat cheese le chèvre *9*
cherry la cerise *3*
chestnut tree le marronnier *2*
children les enfants (*m.pl.*) *7*
china
　Limoges china la porcelaine de
　　Limoges *7*
Chinese chinois(e) *3*
chocolate le chocolat *2*
chocolate mousse la mousse au
　chocolat *2*
to choose choisir *2*
Christmas le Noël *5*

cider le cidre *7*
cigarette la cigarette *7*
cinema le cinéma *2*
circus le cirque *6*
to claim prétendre *7*
class la classe *2*
　coach class (*airplane*) la classe
　　économique *6*
　first class (*airplane, train*)
　　la première class *6*
classical classique *2*
to clean the house faire le ménage *9*
closed fermé(e) *7*
clothing store la boutique de
　vêtements *9*
club le club *6*
clutch (*car*) l'embrayage (*m.*) *8*
coach class (*airplane*) la classe
　économique *6*
cocktail le cocktail *6*
code
　area code l'indicatif (*m.*) *5*
coffee
　black coffee le café noir *4*
　coffee with milk/cream le café
　　crème *4*
coke le coca-cola *4*
cold froid(e) *2*
　cold water l'eau froide (*f.*) *5*
　to be cold avoir froid *3*
　it is cold (weather) il fait froid *2*
to come back rentrer *8*; revenir *9*
to come down descendre *7*
to come from venir de + *noun 9*
　Where do you come from? Vous
　　êtes d'où? *1*
comic strip la bande dessinée *3*
communication (*phone call*)
　la communication *5*
completely tout à fait *6*
compote (*fruit*) la compote *6*
computer l'ordinateur (*m.*) *2*
concert le concert *3*
confirmation la confirmation *5*
content content(e) *3*
convention le congrès *4*
to cook cuisiner *6*; faire la cuisine *9*
it is cool (weather) il fait frais *2*
corridor le couloir *7*

to cost
  it costs ça fait *4*
to count compter *4*
country (*nation*) le pays *7*
countryside la campagne *6*
courageous courageux(-euse) *3*
courtyard
  overlooking the courtyard le côté
    cour *5*
cousin le cousin/la cousine *7*
cream la crème *2*
credit card la carte de crédit *3*
crème brûlée la crème brûlée *2*
crêpe la crêpe *2*
criminal le criminel *6*
croissant le croissant *2*
crushed to pulp (*fruit*) en compote
  6
to cry (*weep*) pleurer *9*
Cuban cubain(e) *3*
cup la tasse *4*

dad, daddy le papa *1*
daily special (*restaurant*) le plat du
  jour *3*
dairy (store) la crémerie *9*
dangerous dangereux(-euse) *3*
dark beer une brune *4*
darling mon chéri/ma chérie *1*
date
  to have a date avoir rendez-vous *3*
daughter la fille *7*
daughter-in-law la belle-fille *6*
day le jour, la journée *5*
  All Saints' Day la Toussaint *5*
  Assumption Day (*August 15*)
    l'Assomption (*f.*) *5*
  feast day la fête *5*
  Have a nice day! Bonne journée! *5*
  New Year's Day le jour de l'An *5*
dead
  to play dead faire le mort *9*
decanter la carafe *4*
December décembre *5*
decision la décision *7*
deli
  gourmet deli le traiteur *9*
delicious délicieux(-euse) *2*
delighted enchanté(e) *1*

dentist le/la dentiste *1*
departure le départ *8*
to desire to vouloir *5*
desk le bureau *2*
  reception desk la réception *5*
dessert le dessert *2*
dessertspoon la petite cuillère,
  la cuillère à dessert *6*
to detest détester *2*
to die mourir *9*
diet le régime *8*
difficult difficile *7*
dining car le wagon-restaurant *9*
dinner le dîner *6*
direction la direction *9*
dish
  to do the dishes faire la vaisselle *9*
  main dish le plat principal *6*
to dislike détester *2*
divorced divorcé(e) *7*
to do faire *2*
  to do the dishes faire la vaisselle *9*
  to do (the) laundry faire la lessive
    9
doctor le docteur *1*
doctor (*female*) la doctoresse *6*
dog le chien *8*
door la porte *5*
double room la chambre double *5*
draft beer la bière pression *4*
to dream rêver *2*
drink la boisson *4*
drugstore la pharmacie *9*
drunk ivre, saoul(e) *9*
dryer
  hair dryer le séchoir à cheveux *5*
duck le canard *6*
duty le service *7*

eager impatient(e) *3*
early en avance *3*
Easter Pâques *5*
to eat manger *2*
economical économique *5*
eight huit *3*
eighteen dix-huit *4*
eighth huitième *7*
eighty quatre-vingts *5*
electrician l'électricien(ne) *1*

eleven onze *3*
emotional émotif(-ive) *3*
to end terminer *2*
English anglais(e) *3*
English Channel la Manche *6*
enough (*sufficiently*) assez *3*
to enter entrer *9*
entirely entièrement *6*
especially surtout *8*
  especially not surtout pas *8*
espresso l'expresso (*m.*) *4*
estate le domaine *9*
European européen(ne) *1*
evening le soir *2;* la soirée *8*
  good evening bonsoir *1*
every tout/toute *7*
excellent excellent(e) *2*
excursion la randonnée *8*
excuse me (*sorry*) excusez-moi,
  pardon *1*
expensive cher/chère *5*
extremely well done (*meat*) bien
  cuit(e) *9*

facecloth le gant de toilette *5*
to face onto donner sur *5*
fall (*season*) l'automne (*m.*) *2*
to fall tomber *9*
family la famille *7*
famous célèbre *6*
far end le fond *7*
far from loin de *6*
fast rapide *8*
father le père *7*
father-in-law le beau-père *7*
feast day la fête *5*
February février *5*
to feel great être en pleine forme *3*
fencing l'escrime (*f.*) *4*
festival le festival *5*
a few quelques *9*
fifteen quinze *4*
fifth cinquième *7*
fifty cinquante *4*
to fill remplir *6*
  Fill up the tank! Faites le plein! *4*
action film le film d'action *2*
finally enfin *4*
to finish finir *6*

first d'abord *4*
first class (*airplane, train*) la première
  classe *6*
first-rate vineyard le cru *9*
fish le poisson *6*
five cinq *3*
floor (*of building*) l'étage (*m.*) *7*
  ground floor le rez-de-chaussée *7*
flower la fleur *2*
fog le brouillard *2*
follow me suivez-moi *6*
for a long time longtemps *9*
foreign étranger(-ère) *8*
to forget oublier *9*
fork la fourchette *6*
forty quarante *4*
four quatre *3*
fourteen quatorze *4*
fourth quatrième *7*
France la France *2*
French (*language*) le français *2*
French (*person*) le Français/
  la Française *2*
fresh (*cheese*) bien frais *9*
  too fresh (*cheese*) trop frais *9*
  fresh lemon juice le citron pressé *4*
Friday vendredi *5*
friend l'ami (*m.*)/l'amie (*f.*) *1*
from de *1*
front
  in front of en face de *6*
fruit pie la tarte aux fruits *2*
fruit salad la salade de fruits *6*
full complet/complète *5*
furious furieux(-euse) *3*

to gain weight grossir *6*
garden le jardin *6*
general
  in general en général *6*
generous généreux(-euse) *3*
Geneva Genève *4*
gentlemen Messieurs *1*
  ladies and gentlemen
    Messieurs-dames *1*
to get in (a car, etc.) monter *4*
to get up se lever *9*
gift store les souvenirs-cadeaux
  (*m.pl.*) *9*

girl la fille *2*
to give a kiss faire un bisou *4*
to give up, to give back rendre *7*
glass le verre *4*
to go aller *2*
to go down descendre *7*
to go for a ride faire un tour *4*
to go shopping faire des courses *9;*
faire du shopping *4*
to go through passer par *8*
to go to the bathroom aller aux
toilettes *4*
to go up monter *4*
goat la chèvre *9*
  goat cheese le chèvre *9*
good bon/bonne *2*
  good evening, good-bye bonsoir *1*
  good morning, good afternoon
bonjour *1*
  good night bonne nuit *1*
good-bye au revoir *1;*
(*Switzerland/Canada*) adieu *1*
gourmand (*food-loving*) gourmand(e)
6
gourmet deli le traiteur *9*
granddaughter la petite-fille *7*
grandfather le grand-père *7*
grandmother la grand-mère *7*
grandparents les grands-parents
(*m.pl.*) *7*
grandson le petit-fils *7*
grapefruit le pamplemousse *4*
great grand(e) *3*
  to feel great être en pleine forme *3*
green vert(e) *3*
grilled ham-and-cheese sandwich
le croque-monsieur *6*
grocer's, grocery l'épicerie (*f.*) *9*
ground floor le rez-de-chaussée *7*
grove le/les bois *3*
to grow grandir *6*
guest l'invité(e) *6*
guitar la guitare *2*
gymnastics la gymnastique *6*

hair les cheveux (*m.pl.*) *3*
hair dryer le séchoir à cheveux *5*
half demi(e) *4*
hall le couloir *7*

ham le jambon *4*
  grilled ham-and-cheese sandwich
le croque-monsieur *6*
hand la main *9*
hand towel la serviette de toilette *5*
happy heureux(-euse), content(e) *3*
to have avoir *3*
  Have a nice day! Bonne journée!
5
  to have just accomplished
something venir de + *verb* *9*
to have to devoir + *verb* *5*
he il *1*
headwaiter le maître d'hôtel *6*
to hear entendre *7*
heavy lourd(e) *3*
hello (*good morning, good afternoon*)
bonjour *1;* (*good evening*) bonsoir
1
to help aider *5*
hence donc *8*
her son/sa/ses *7*
here
  here is voici, voilà *2*
  here it is la voici *4*
  was not here n'était pas ici *7*
hero le héros *3*
herself elle *4*
hey eh *2*
hi salut *1*
high haut(e) *3*
high-speed train le Train à Grande
Vitesse (le TGV) *8*
highway l'autoroute (*f.*) *7*
his son/sa/ses *7*
historic historique *2*
holiday le jour férié *5*
  holidays les vacances (*f.pl.*) *3*
home
  at the home of chez *9*
  Make yourself at home. Faites
comme chez vous. *4*
homework le devoir *6*
horn la sirène *7*
hors d'oeuvre le hors-d'œuvre *6*
hot chaud(e) *2*
hot water l'eau chaude (*f.*) *5*
hotel l'hôtel (*m.*) *3*
hotel room la chambre *5*

hour l'heure (*f.*) *3*
in the morning hours la matinée *8*
house la maison *6*
to clean the house faire le ménage *9*
household appliance l'électroménager (*m.*) *9*
how comment *8*
How are you? (*familiar*) Ça va? *1*; (*formal*) Comment allez-vous? *1*
How come? Comment cela? *5*
How much is it? C'est combien? *4*
How old are you? Quel âge as-tu? *3*
huge énorme *3*
one hundred cent *5*
hungry
to be hungry avoir faim *3*
to hurry faire vite *9*
to be in a hurry être pressé(e) *3*
I am in a hurry je suis pressé(e) *1*
husband le mari *7*
Hush! Chut! *9*

I je *1*; moi *2*
ice la glace *4*
black ice le verglas *2*
ice cream la glace *4*
icy glacé(e) *6*
ID card la carte d'identité *9*
idea l'idée (*f.*) *2*
idealistic idéaliste *3*
to idolize adorer *2*
impatient impatient(e) *3*
the important thing l'important (*m.*) *8*
impossible impossible *5*
impulsive impulsif(-ive) *3*
in à *1*; en *2*
in front of devant *6*
in love amoureux(-euse) *3*
independent indépendant(e) *3*
ink (ballpoint) pen le stylo *2*
intelligent intelligent(e) *3*
interesting intéressant(e) *3*
Internet l'Internet (*m.*) *5*
to introduce présenter *1*
introduction la présentation *1*
to invite inviter *6*

ironing le repassage *6*
irritable irritable *3*
it (*m.*)/it (*f.*) il/elle *1*
it costs ça fait *4*
it is c'est *3*
Italian italien(ne) *3*
Italy l'Italie (*f.*) *1*
its (*possessive*) son/sa/ses *7*

January janvier *5*
Japanese japonais(e) *3*
jet lag le décalage horaire *4*
jewelry store la bijouterie *9*
job (*position*) le poste *3*
journalist le/la journaliste *1*
judge le juge *6*
juice le jus *4*
fresh lemon juice le citron pressé *4*
July juillet *5*
June juin *5*

karate le karaté *4*
key la clé *5*
kind aimable *3*
kir (*aperitif*) le kir *4*
kiss le bisou (*colloquial*) *4*
to give a kiss faire un bisou *4*
knife le couteau *6*
to know (I know) savoir (je sais) *8*; connaître *8*

ladies and gentlemen Messieurs-dames *1*
lag
jet lag le décalage horaire *4*
lager une blonde *4*
lakeside (*village or home*) lacustre *9*
late tard *6*
to be late être en retard *3*
later plus tard *7*
see you later à tout à l'heure *1*
laundromat la laverie automatique *9*
to do (the) laundry faire la lessive *9*
to learn apprendre *4*
leave (*vacation*) le congé *7*
on leave (*vacation*) en congé *7*
to leave partir *6*
Don't leave me. Ne me quitte pas. *1*

left
   to the left à gauche *7*
lemon le citron *4*
   fresh lemon juice le citron pressé *4*
lemonade le citron pressé *4*
library la bibliothèque *4*
to light allumer *9*
light switch l'interrupteur (*m.*) *5*
lightbulb l'ampoule (*f.*) *5*
like (*as*) comme *3*
to like aimer *2*
Limoges china la porcelaine de
   Limoges *7*
to listen (to) écouter *2*
a little un peu *2*
to live (somewhere) habiter *2*
lobster le homard *3*
local wine le vin du pays *9*
London Londres *4*
long long(ue) *3*
   for a long time longtemps *9*
long live vive *9*
to look (at) regarder *2*
to look like ressembler à *7*
to lose perdre *7*
to lose weight maigrir *6*
a lot beaucoup (de) *5*
lottery ticket le billet de loterie *5*
love l'amour (*m.*) *1*
   in love amoureux(-euse) *3*
to love aimer *2*; (*to idolize*) adorer *2*
lucky
   to be lucky avoir de la chance *3*
lunch le déjeuner *6*

mad (*crazy*) fou/folle *3*
madam (mesdames) Madame
   (Mesdames) *1*
magical magique *6*
magnificent magnifique *9*
main dish le plat principal *6*
maître d' le maître d'hôtel *6*
to make faire *2*
   Make yourself at home. Faites
      comme chez vous. *4*
mama, mom la maman *1*
man l'homme (*m.*) *3*
many beaucoup (de) *5*
map la carte *3*

March mars *5*
match (*sports*) le match *2*
matter
   It does not matter. Ça ne fait rien.
      4
   What does it matter? Qu'est-ce que
      ça peut faire? *8*
May mai *5*
maybe peut-être *9*
meal le repas *6*
to mean vouloir dire *7*
mechanic le mécanicien/
   la mécanicienne *1*
medical médical(e) *4*
medicine (*field of study*) la médecine
   1
medium rare (*meat*) saignant(e) *9*
Melba
   peach Melba (*dessert*) la pêche
      Melba *2*
mention
   Don't mention it. De rien. *1*
to meow miauler *8*
Mexican mexicain(e) *3*
midday midi *4*
middle
   in the middle of au milieu de *6*
midnight minuit *4*
milk le lait *4*
   coffee with milk le café au lait *4*
mind (*spirit*) l'esprit (*m.*) *3*
mineral water l'eau minérale (*f.*) *4*;
   (*sparkling, carbonated*) l'eau
   gazeuse/pétillante (*f.*) *4*; (*still,
   noncarbonated*) l'eau plate (*f.*) *4*
mint la menthe *4*
a minute un instant *4*
miss (*young lady*) Mademoiselle *1*
misses (*young ladies*) Mesdemoiselles
   1
mist la brume *2*
modern moderne *3*
mom la maman *1*
Monday lundi *5*
month le mois *5*
monument le monument *2*
moon la lune *6*
more plus, encore *5*
   one more time encore une fois *5*

morning le matin *2*
  good morning bonjour *1*
  the morning hours la matinée *8*
Morocco le Maroc *6*
mortadella (*cold cut*) la mortadelle *9*
Moscow Moscou *4*
mother la mère *7*
mother-in-law la belle-mère *7*
Mr. Monsieur *1*
Mrs. Madame, Mesdames *1*
much beaucoup (de) *5*
  very much beaucoup *2*
muscular musclé(e) *3*
museum le musée *1*
music la musique *7*
must devoir + *verb 5*
mustache la moustache *3*
mustard la moutarde *6*
my mon/ma/mes *1*
myself (*for my part*) moi *2*

name le nom *5*
  my name is _____ je m'appelle
  _____ *1*
  What is your name? Comment
  vous appelez-vous? *1*
nap
  to take a nap faire la sieste *4*
napkin la serviette de table *6*
nature la nature *2*
near près de *6*
to need avoir besoin de/d' *5*
  need not be made n'est plus à faire
  6
neither non plus *6*
  neither do I moi non plus *6*
nephew le neveu *7*
new neuf/neuve *3*
New Orleans la Nouvelle-Orléans *4*
New Year's Day le jour de l'An *5*
next prochain(e) *3;* ensuite *4*
next to à côté de *6*
nice
  it is nice (weather) il fait beau *2*
niece la nièce *7*
night la nuit *2*
  good night bonne nuit *1*
nine neuf *3*
nineteen dix-neuf *4*

ninety quatre-vingt-dix *5*
ninth neuvième *7*
no non *1*
noncarbonated mineral water l'eau
  plate *4*
noon midi *4*
notebook le cahier *2*
nothing rien *7*
November novembre *5*
now maintenant *8*
number le numéro *5*

to obey obéir à *5*
October octobre *5*
of de *1*
off
  to be off (*on leave*) être en congé *7*
often souvent *2*
okay d'accord *4*
old
  How old are you? Quel âge as-tu?
  3
omelet l'omelette (*f.*) *6*
on sur *2*
  to be on leave être en congé *7*
one (*number*) un *3*
onion l'oignon (*m.*) *6*
only seulement *5*
open, opened ouvert(e) *7*
  open ticket (*train*) le billet ouvert
  8
to open onto donner sur *5*
optimistic optimiste *3*
or ou *2*
orange l'orange (*f.*) *2*
to order commander *2*
other autre *8*
our notre/nos *7*
ourselves nous *4*
outside dehors *9*
over here par ici *6*
overlooking the courtyard/street
  le côté cour/rue *5*
overripe (*cheese*) trop fait *9*
to owe devoir + *noun 5*

painting la peinture *9*
  rock painting la peinture rupestre
  9

pale ale une blonde *4*
pancake la crêpe *2*
paper
   toilet paper le papier hygiénique *5*
parents les parents (*m.pl.*) *7*
parents-in-law les beaux-parents (*m.pl.*) *7*
Parisian parisien(ne) *4*
particularly en particulier *9*
party la fête *5*
to pass passer *4*
passerby le passant/la passante *7*
passport le passeport *5*
pastry la pâtisserie *2*
to pay payer *4*
peach Melba (*dessert*) la pêche Melba *2*
pear la poire *4*
pen
   ink (ballpoint) pen le stylo *2*
pencil le crayon *2*
Pentecost la Pentecôte *5*
pepper le poivre *6*
perfume le parfum *7*
perhaps peut-être *9*
person la personne *3*
pharmacy la pharmacie *9*
to phone téléphoner *5*
phone call l'appel (*m.*), la communication *5*
phone card la télécarte *5*
photo la photo *4*
to photograph photographier *8*
to pick up cueillir *3*
picnic le pique-nique *9*
pie la tarte *4*
   fruit pie la tarte aux fruits *2*
pillow l'oreiller (*m.*) *5*
pineapple l'ananas (*m.*) *4*
pizza la pizza *4*
place setting le couvert *6*
plane l'avion (*m.*) *5*
planet la planète *5*
plate l'assiette (*f.*) *6*
to play jouer *2*
   to play dead faire le mort *9*
   to play (*practice*) a sport faire du sport *4*

please s'il te plaît (*familiar sing.*) *4;* s'il vous plaît (*pl. and formal sing.*) *4*
pleasure le plaisir *2*
plumber le plombier *1*
to ponder réfléchir *6*
pork butcher's shop la charcuterie *9*
position (*job*) le poste *3*
positive positif(-ive) *3*
possibility la possibilité *3*
post office la poste *9*
to prefer préférer *8*
preferred préféré(e) *2*
prehistory la préhistoire *8*
president le président/la présidente *2*
problem le problème *5*
professor le professeur *1*
psychoanalytical psychanalytique *3*
to punch a ticket composter *8*
to punish punir *6*
to put (on) mettre *9*

quarter past (*time*) et quart *4*
quarter to (*time*) moins le quart *4*

rabbit le lapin *6*
race la course *6*
to rain pleuvoir *2*
   it rains, it's raining il pleut *2*
raincoat l'imperméable (*m.*), le manteau de pluie *9*
rare
   medium rare (*meat*) siagnant(e) *9*
   very rare (*meat*) bleu(e) *9*
raspberry la framboise *4*
raw (*like steak tartare*) cru(e) *9*
raw vegetables les crudités (*f.pl.*) *6*
razor le rasoir *5*
really vraiment *9*
reception desk la réception *5*
receptionist le/la réceptionniste *1*
red rouge *3*
   all red toutes rouges *3*
region la région *8*
relatives les parents (*m.pl.*) *7*
to rent louer *8*
rental la location *8*
to represent représenter *3*

republic la république *9*
reputation la renommée *6*
require
 did it require? a-t-il fallu? *7*
research scientist le chercheur/
 la chercheuse *9*
reservation la réservation *3*
to reserve réserver *2*
resourceful astucieux(-euse) *3*
restaurant le restaurant *2*
return le retour *8*
to return rentrer; retourner *8*
rich riche *7*
ride
 to go for a ride faire un tour *4*
right
 to the right à droite *7*
ring le rond *9*
ripe (*cheese*) bien fait *9*
 overripe (*cheese*) trop fait *9*
road la route *2*
road ice le verglas *2*
robber le brigand *9*
rock painting la peinture rupestre *9*
room la chambre *5*
 air-conditioned room la chambre
 climatisée *5*
 double room la chambre double *5*
 single room la chambre simple *5*
rooster le coq *1*
round-trip ticket aller et retour *8*

sailing la voile *4*
saint
 All Saints' Day la Toussaint *5*
Saint Helena (*island*) Sainte-Hélène
 9
salad la salade *2*
 fruit salad la salade de fruits *6*
 salad dressing la sauce *4*
salami le saucisson sec *4*
salt le sel *6*
sandwich le sandwich *4*
 grilled ham-and-cheese sandwich
 le croque-monsieur *6*
Saturday samedi *5*
sauce la sauce *4*
saucer la soucoupe *6*
sauna le sauna *5*

sausage la saucisse *4*
to say dire *7*
 that is to say c'est-à-dire *6*
schoolbag le sac, le cartable *2*
sea la mer *2*
second deuxième *7*
secretary le/la secrétaire *1*
to see voir *7*
 see you later à tout à l'heure *1*
 see you soon à bientôt *1*
 see you tomorrow à demain *1*
selfish égoïste *3*
to sell vendre *7*
September septembre *5*
to serve servir *6*
service le service *7*
setting
 place setting le couvert *6*
seven sept *3*
seventeen dix-sept *4*
seventh septième *7*
seventy soixante-dix *5*
she elle *1*
sheet (*of paper*) la feuille *2*
sherbet le sorbet *2*
shift car (*with manual transmission*)
 la voiture à embrayage *8*
shoe la chaussure *7*
shop
 butcher's shop la boucherie *9*
 pork butcher's shop la charcuterie
 9
 tobacco shop le bureau de tabac *5*
shopping
 to go shopping faire des courses *9*;
 faire du shopping *4*
short (*not for people*) court(e) *3*
show (*sight, performance*) le spectacle
 7
shower la douche *5*
 to take a shower prendre la douche
 5
shrimp la crevette *6*
shy timide *3*
sick malade *3*
side le côté *5*
sight (*show*) le spectacle *7*
sincere sincère *3*
single room la chambre simple *5*

sir Monsieur *1*
siren la sirène *7*
sister la sœur *7*
sister-in-law la belle-sœur *7*
six six *3*
sixteen seize *4*
sixth sixième *7*
sixty soixante *4*
ski le ski *2*
to ski skier *2*
skiing le ski *2*
to sleep dormir *6*
sleepy
  to be sleepy avoir sommeil *3*
slice la tranche *9*
small petit(e) *3*
smoke la fumée *9*
to smoke fumer *5*
snail l'escargot (*m.*) *6*
to snow neiger *2*
so do I moi aussi *2*
so-so comme ci comme ça *1*
soap
  bath soap la savonnette *5*
soccer le football *4*
sociable sociable *3*
soda le soda *7*
some quelques *9*
sometimes quelquefois *3*
son le fils *7*
son-in-law le gendre *7*
soon bientôt *2*
  see you soon à bientôt *1*
sorry désolé(e) *5*
sorry (*excuse me*) excusez-moi,
  pardon *1*
soup la soupe *6*
spaghetti les spaghettis *4*
Spanish espagnol(e) *3*
sparkling mineral water l'eau
  gazeuse/pétillante (*f.*) *4*
to speak parler *2*
speech le discours *2*
speed la vitesse *8*
speleology la spéléologie *9*
spirit (*mind*) l'esprit (*m.*) *3*
splendid magnifique *9*
spoken word la parole *9*
spoon la cuillère/la cuiller *6*

sport
  to play a sport faire du sport *4*
spring le printemps *2*
stalactite la stalactite *9*
to stand up se lever *9*
to start commencer *2*
to starve mourir de faim *9*
station (*train*) la gare *4*
to stay rester *4*
step-brother le demi-frère *7*
step-sister la demi-sœur *7*
still encore *5*
still mineral water l'eau plate (*f.*) *4*
to stir tourner *9*
storm l'orage (*m.*) *2*
store
  antique store l'antiquaire (*m.*) *4*
  bookstore la librairie *9*
  clothing store la boutique de
    vêtements *9*
  dairy store la crémerie *9*
  drugstore la pharmacie *9*
  gift store les souvenirs-cadeaux
    (*m.pl.*) *9*
  grocery l'épicerie (*f.*) *9*
  jewelry store la bijouterie *9*
  supermarket le supermarché *9*
stout beer une brune *4*
straight droit(e) *3*
  straight ahead tout droit *7*
strawberry la fraise *4*
strawberry milkshake le lait-fraise *4*
street la rue *7*
  overlooking the street le côté rue *5*
to stroll se promener *7*
strong fort(e) *3*
student l'étudiant (*m.*); l'étudiante
  (*f.*) *1*
study l'étude (*f.*) *3*
to study étudier *2*
subway le métro *7*
to succeed réussir *6*
sufficiently (*enough*) assez *3*
summer l'été (*m.*) *2*
Sunday dimanche *5*
superb magnifique *9*
supermarket le supermarché *9*
sure
  to be sure être sûr(e) *3*

surprised surpris(e) *8*
swallow (*bird*) l'hirondelle (*f.*) *2*
Swedish suédois(e) *3*
to swim nager *2*
swimming la natation *4*
switch
   light switch l'interrupteur (*m.*) *5*

table la table *2*
tablecloth la nappe *6*
tablespoon la cuillère à soupe *6*
to take prendre *4*
   did it take? a-t-il fallu? *7*
   to take a nap faire la sieste *4*
   to take a shower prendre une
     douche *5*
   to take a walk faire une promenade
     4
tall grand(e) *3*
tart (*pie*) la tarte *4*
taxi le taxi *4*
tea (*plain*) le thé nature *4*
teacher le professeur *1*
teaspoon la cuillère à café *6*
technician le technicien/
   la technicienne *1*
tee-shirt le tee-shirt *7*
telephone le téléphone *3*
to telephone téléphoner *5*
television, TV la télévision, la télé
   2
to tell dire *7*
ten dix *3*
tennis le tennis *2*
tenth dixième *7*
terrace la terrasse *1*
thank you merci *1*
that ce/cette *5*; ça *6*; qui *3*
that is to say c'est-à-dire *6*
theater le théâtre *5*
their leur/leurs *7*
themselves elles, eux *1*
then alors *2*; ensuite *4*; donc *8*
there is, there are voilà *2*
therefore donc *8*
these ces *8*
they ils (*m.pl.*), elles (*f.pl.*) *1*
to think penser *7*
third troisième *7*

thirsty
   to be thirsty avoir soif *3*
thirteen treize *4*
thirty trente *4*
this ce/cette *5*
this way par ici *6*
those ces *8*
one thousand mille *5*
three trois *3*
through à travers *8*
Thursday jeudi *5*
ticket le billet *2*
   lottery ticket le billet de loterie *5*
   open ticket (*train*) le billet ouvert
     8
   to punch a ticket composter *8*
   round-trip ticket aller et retour *8*
time le temps *2*; l'heure (*f.*) *3*
   for a long time longtemps *9*
   one more time encore une fois *5*
   What time is it? Quelle heure est-il?
     3
timid timide *3*
tip (*in a restaurant*) le pourboire *4*
tired fatigué(e) *1*
to à *1*
tobacco shop le bureau de tabac *5*
today aujourd'hui *8*
together ensemble *2*
toilet les toilettes (*f.pl.*) *4*
toilet paper le papier hygiénique *5*
toiletries les effets de toilette (*m.pl.*)
   5
tomato la tomate *4*
tomorrow demain *5*
   see you tomorrow à demain *1*
too fresh (*cheese*) trop frais *9*
toothbrush la brosse à dents *5*
toothpaste le dentifrice *5*
total le total *3*
totally entièrement *6*
tourist le/la touriste *5*
towel
   bath towel la serviette de bain *5*
   hand towel la serviette de toilette *5*
tower la tour *4*
train le train *4*
   high-speed train le Train à Grande
     Vitesse (le TGV) *8*

to travel voyager *2*
too fresh (*cheese*) trop frais *9*
travel agency l'agence de voyages (*f.*) *8*
travel agent le/la voyagiste *8*
trip le voyage *2*
true vrai(e) *4*
truly vraiment *9*
Tunisia la Tunisie *5*
Tunisian tunisien(ne) *3*
twelve douze *3*
twenty vingt *4*
two deux *3*

umbrella le parapluie *6*
uncle l'oncle (*m.*) *7*
under sous *6*
to understand comprendre *4*
unhappy malheureux(-euse) *3*
us nous *4*
to use utiliser *5*

vacation les vacances (*f.pl.*) *3*
  on vacation en congé *7*
vain vaniteux(-euse) *3*
vanilla la vanille *2*
vegetables
  raw vegetables les crudités (*f.pl.*) *6*
very much beaucoup *2*
very rare (*close to raw; meat*) bleu(e) *9*
veterinarian le/la vétérinaire *1*
victory la victoire *5*
vineyard
  first-rate vineyard le cru *9*
to visit (*a place*) visiter *2*

to wait for attendre *7*
waiter le garçon *2*; le serveur *7*
waitress la serveuse *6*
to walk marcher *2*
  to take a walk faire une promenade *4*
  to walk leisurely se promener *7*
to want désirer *4*; vouloir *5*
warm chaud(e) *2*
  to be warm avoir chaud *3*
  it is warm (*weather*) il fait chaud *2*
warm-hearted chaleureux(-euse) *3*

to warn avertir *6*
washcloth le gant de toilette *5*
water l'eau (*f.*) *4*
  cold water l'eau froide (*f.*) *5*
  hot water l'eau chaude (*f.*) *5*
  mineral water l'eau minérale (*f.*) *4*
we nous *1*
wealthy riche *7*
weather le temps *2*
  it is bad (*weather*) il fait mauvais *2*
  it is cold (*weather*) il fait froid *2*
  it is cool (*weather*) il fait frais *2*
  it is nice (*weather*) il fait beau *2*
  it is warm (*weather*) il fait chaud *2*
  What is the weather like? Quel temps fait-il? *2*
Wednesday mercredi *5*
week la semaine *5*
weekend le week-end *6*
weight
  to gain weight grossir *6*
  to lose weight maigrir *6*
welcome
  you are welcome de rien *1*; à votre service *7*
well bien *1*; eh bien *2*; ben (*slang for* bien) *7*
  extremely well done (*meat*) bien cuit(e) *9*
what quoi *6*; quel(le) *2*
what? qu'est-ce que/qu'? *2*
  What? (*How come?*) Comment cela? *5*
  What does it matter? Qu'est-ce que ça peut faire? *8*
  What is it? Qu'est-ce que c'est? *3*
  What is the weather like? Quel temps fait-il? *2*
  what is there? qu'est-ce qui y'a? (*colloquial*) *7*
  What is your name? Comment vous appelez-vous? *1*
  What time is it? Quelle heure est-il? *3*
where où *1*
  Where do you come from? Vous êtes d'où? *1*
which quel(le) *2*; qui *3*

white blanc/blanche *4*
Whitsuntide la Pentecôte *5*
who qui *3*
  Who is he/she? Qui est-ce?, Qui c'est?, Qui est-ce que c'est? *3*
Why not? Pourquoi pas? *2*
wife la femme *4*
will be seront *3*
window la fenêtre *5*
windy
  it is windy il fait du vent *2*
wine le vin *4*
  local wine le vin du pays *9*
  wine cellar la cave à vin *8*
  wine merchant le marchand de vin *9*
winter l'hiver (*m.*) *2*
to wish désirer *4*; vouloir *5*
with avec *2*
without sans *5*
woman la femme *4*
wonderland le pays des merveilles *6*
wood(s) le/les bois *3*
word
  spoken word la parole *9*
work le travail *5*

to work travailler *2*
worldwide mondial(e) *6*
worry
  Don't worry. Ne vous en faites pas. *4*
worth
  it is worth it ça vaut le coup (de) *9*
  it is worth the effort ça vaut la peine de *9*

year l'année (*f.*) *3*
yellow jaune *3*
yes oui *2*
yesterday hier *7*
yet encore *5*
you tu (*familiar sing.*) *1*; (*pl. or formal sing.*) vous *1*
young ladies Mesdemoiselles *1*
your ton/ta/tes (*familiar*) *7*; votre/vos (*pl. or formal sing.*) *7*
yourself/yourselves toi (*familiar sing.*) *4*; vous (*pl. or formal sing.*) *4*
youth la jeunesse *7*

zero zéro *3*